# WEEKEND Decorator!

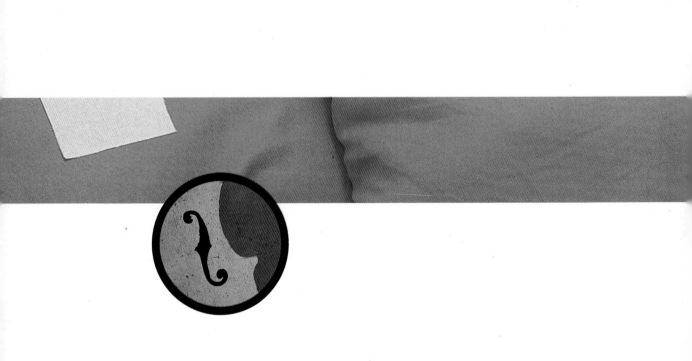

# WEEKEND Decorator!

HOW TO TRANSFORM A ROOM IN A WEEKEND

# THE BOOK OF THE HIT TV SERIES

HarperCollins*Publishers*

First published in 1998 by HarperCollins*Publishers*
in association with Granada Television Limited

Text © 1998 Granada Television Limited
Design and layout © 1998 HarperCollins*Publishers*

A catalogue record for this book is available
from the British Library.

ISBN 0 00 414037 0

For HarperCollins*Publishers:*
**Editor:** Becky Humphreys
**Designer:** Paul Calver
**Production:** Matt Bourne
**Location Photographer:** Shona Wood
**Location Photography Stylist:** Jane Forster
**Indexer:** Sue Bosanko

For This Morning:
**Producer:** Susan McDermott
**Director:** Ann Walsh
**Editor:** Helen Williams
**Researchers:** Simone Pilkington, Joanna Bennett-Coles

**Decorators:** Gary Allson, Kristina Clackson, Ashleigh
Downey, Claire King, Nikki King, Charlotte Lefley,
Prem Mistry and Annabell Norden.

**Additional picture credits:** David Carter by James
Mortimer (page 8); Stewart Walton by Graham Rae
(page 9); crackle-glazing technique by Flavio Galozzi
(Robert Harding Syndication); gilding brush
by Steve Tanner (Robert Harding Syndication).

Colour reproduction in Singapore by Colourscan
Printed and bound in Italy

# CONTENTS

# Davina McCall

It all started when I received a telephone call from 'This Morning'. They asked; "Did I like decorating?". The answer was that I liked the results of decorating, I liked watching programmes and reading books on decorating... but I couldn't actually do it myself. Did I want to learn? Yes, I did. I decided that a few interior skills could stand me in good stead if all else failed... a girl can never have too many strings to her bow.

Kitted out in natty Weekend Decorator overalls, and with brushes in hand, we set forth. The big white Weekend Decorator van was a wonderful sight and drew attention wherever we went. It carried us, and a tremendous amount of tools and equipment, all around the country – from Brighouse to Bude and from Dyfed to Middlesex, leaving a trail of brightly-coloured paint behind us.

I have some very happy memories of Weekend Decorator. My favourite was hearing the distant sound of singing from one of the rooms and discovering the team painting and stapling in chorus – a wonderful memory and a great way to get through a lot of hard work. Stripping 7 or 8 layers of wallpaper using steam strippers and then finding that the walls were too wet for the paint to dry was not such a happy memory.

I want to thank all the home owners who gave 'This Morning' their rooms to make-over. It was an amazing show of trust as these people had very little say on the end results.

Decorating a room in a weekend is an ambitious project, so don't be fooled by how easy our team of experts and workers made it look. It was hard work and extremely long hours. The good news is that if you are prepared and have everything you could possibly need, and more just in case, it can be achieved.

And finally, a few handy tips, gleaned from decorating 10 rooms in 5 weeks:

• Don't set your sights too high.

• Choose colours and schemes that will radically change the room without much effort – just a new colour will make you feel like a dramatic change has taken place.

• Keep the weekend solely for decorating by preparing the room in advance. All wallpaper stripping should be done in advance.

• Clean the room and remove everything, if possible. Cover anything you can't move.

• Be radical when it comes to flooring. Be prepared to chuck out old carpets, but be warned about echo, echo, echo on wooden floors.

• Taking time to fill in cracks and holes with polyfiller will make a huge difference to the finished result.

• Get a good group of friends, the phone number of the local pizza delivery, lots of coffee and chocolate biscuits and be prepared to shut yourselves away from the outside world until late Sunday evening...

And finally – Good Luck!

# The Interior Designers

## David Carter

David Carter spent several years working on fashion magazines before a feature on his London home in 'The World of Interiors' brought his decorating skills to the public eye. Such was the interest in his work that he launched his own highly successful interior design business.

Consistently interesting, his work regularly appears in leading newspapers and magazines, both here and abroad, and his first book, *The Complete Paint Book* was recently published by Conran Octopus. Much of his spare time is spent restoring his early eighteenth century house in London's East End, and looking after his baby daughter, Isadora.

## Jocasta Innes

Jocasta Innes was born in Nanking, China, and educated at Bedford High School before winning a place at Girton College, Cambridge, where she read modern languages. After graduating she worked on the London 'Evening Standard', and started writing books. In the past 15 years she has written over 20 books, including *The Paupers Cookbook, Country Kitchen* and *Paint Magic*, which has sold over a million copies worldwide.

She went on to become the design and food editor of 'Cosmopolitan' magazine and in 1986, wrote and presented 'Paintability', a five-part series for Channel 4. Since then Jocasta has written numerous articles for newspapers and magazines and has appeared on television and radio, most notably in her 1996, eight-part, prime-time series on home decoration. She has written, lectured and broadcast extensively on interior design and is currently one of the best-known names in this field.

Jocasta and her team started the Paint Magic Company in February 1993, which includes a mail order and decorating and design service, and in 1996 she launched her own wallpaper and border collection.

## Marta Nowicka

After graduating with an Honours degree in Interior Design from Kingston University in 1988, Marta was recruited by JBP Design Group where she worked for the next five years. Starting as a junior designer, she was quickly promoted to a position as an Associate, in charge of four design teams working for 5-8 clients at any one time. At JBP Design Group Marta's clients included Midland Bank, Merrill Lynch and Mercury Communications. She was also responsible for the design of the OXO building atrium.

Marta's ambition to start her own practice led her to leave JBP and set up as an independent consultant in 1993. At this time she was approached by the University of Central England to act as Senior Lecturer on the BA Interior Design course. Her independent projects have included the redesign of The English National Opera bars and the Body Shop retail outlets. In 1995, Marta founded the Nowicka Stern partnership with Oded Stern-Meiraz.

Marta's work has featured in many magazines and journals including: 'Designer's Journal', 'Building Design', 'Interior Designer', 'Architects Journal', 'Options', 'Time Out', 'Sunday Times' and 'Homes & Garden'.

### Lesley Taylor

Prior to moving into television, Lesley was a working interior designer and had the honour of being made the first full member of the Interior Decorator and Designers Association. Her television career began in 1990 when she undertook a number of interior design items on the 'People Today' programme. This was followed by a ten-week series for Channel 4 Wales.

Regular viewers of 'This Morning' will recognise Lesley from her live appearances with Richard and Judy. Lesley has also presented many television and radio shows about subjects other than interior design, including a series called 'Baby Talk' which covers all aspects of pregnancy, birth and childcare, and a prime time magazine show called 'Don't Look Back'.

Lesley has just begun to write her fifth interior design-based book, and she often writes for interior design magazines such as 'Ideal Home', 'Homeflair' and 'Perfect Home'.

### Stewart Walton

Stewart studied graphic design, fine art and illustration, and one of his first commissions after graduating from the Royal College of Art was to illustrate a cookery book for Jocasta Innes. They then went on to collaborate on 'Paint Magic' and 'Paintability', which became the name of their stencil design company. The stencils are bestsellers worldwide.

Stewart's interest in interior design gradually took over from his work as a college lecturer and freelance graphic designer when commissions started to come in from magazines, publishers and private clients. One of his most exciting interior design jobs was the Windsor home of Billy Connolly and Pamela Stephenson, where he started by designing the gates to the entrance and worked his way right through the house.

He has appeared regularly on television, both here and in the United States, and works in partnership with his wife, Sally, producing books on crafts and decorating – mostly project-based – that concentrate on providing ideas, inspiration and encouragement to get people involved with hands-on creativity.

### Catherine Woram

After gaining an Honours degree in Fashion Communication and Promotions from St Martin's School of Art, followed by a Masters degree from the Royal College of Art, Catherine started working as a fashion stylist and writer.

She moved on to become a shopping editor and then a home interiors stylist, working freelance for many magazines and newspapers including the 'Telegraph' magazine, 'Sunday Mirror', 'Prima', 'Good Food' and 'Homes and Ideas', where she is now the Homes and Design Editor.

Catherine is the author of *Wedding Dress Style*, and contributed to *Contemporary Fashion* and the *Hamlyn Book of Soft Furnishings*.

We chose 10 very different rooms, from 10 very different houses, to show you that you can transform your home, whatever its style or age. Too often books and magazines feature the most beautiful rooms, ready-supplied with gorgeous fireplaces, high ceilings and windows offering stunning views. It's very easy to make a room look wonderful if it already has these features. But for most of us, we need a little more imagination to make our homes interesting, especially if we live in a modern building.

The rooms in this book are not complete kits. Few of us have the space for a music room or a study, for example, but what we hope is that this book will give you plenty of ideas. You may want to decorate a whole room, such as the people featured in this book did, or you may just want to change a small part of it – either way, there are ideas and techniques to help.

## Hallway

Jocasta Innes transformed a typical, turn-of-the-century London terrace house hallway for Sarah and Chris Stonelaw.

## Lounge

Stewart Walton was faced with the challenge of decorating a large, London lounge for four young men.

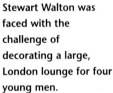

## Master bedroom

Lesley Taylor was asked to create a romantic bedroom for Shirley and Bill Diamond. They live in Cardiff, overlooking the Severn.

## Child's bedroom

Stewart Walton went to Manchester to decorate Rachel's (aged 11) bedroom. She was fed up with flowery wallpaper!

# Introduction

## Kitchen

Catherine Woram added a welcome dose of colour and style to a standard, modern kitchen, without spending a fortune.

## Dining room

Marta Nowicka decorated a dining room in a large, family house situated by the sea in Bude, north Cornwall.

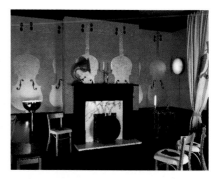

## Music room

David Carter travelled to Brighouse in West Yorkshire to change Pat and Wendy O'Connor's spare room into a music room.

## Children's playroom

Lesley Taylor went to Bury Port in Wales to convert an under-used loft into a beautiful (and fun) playroom for three young children.

## Study

Catherine Woram was asked to make a small, crowded room in Old Isleworth, Middlesex, into a study and a spare bedroom.

## Bathroom

Jocasta Innes helped Battersea couple Zoey and James Hines to transform their *en suite* bathroom. It now looks much more welcoming.

Stencils were used in many of the rooms, including words in the kitchen (*left*) and giant violins in the music room (*opposite*).

## Design

Some of the ideas featured in the book are very specific – the fish motif in the kitchen, for example (above), but what it shows is how you can take an idea or theme that is personal to you, and make a bold design from it. This may result in an entirely themed room, such as the train station playroom, or in a less obvious way, such as the wine names written on the dining room fireplace (below right).

If you are thinking of decorating a whole room, it is often a good idea to buy one or two good quality items to give a theme and structure to the room. This could be something like a new, stylish sofa. You can take the colour and structure of the sofa to work out a scheme for the room. Or you could work around something more dramatic, such as the drums in the music room.

## Colour

Be brave – be bold! Many of the rooms in this book use bold, bright colours such as orange and purple, and they look great. If we'd told our homeowners what colours we were going to use, many of them would have looked very worried, but everyone was delighted with the finished rooms. One fear people have is that a colour will date, and they shy away from bold, dramatic colours, thinking that they will go out of fashion, or that they will tire of them. This may be true, but it's also the same with 'safer', paler colours. Do you remember when everyone had pastel pink, beige and peach walls? Now a room painted in those colours would look dated. If you don't feel confident using bold colours on walls, why not ring the changes with soft furnishings such as throws and cushions or by painting your existing furniture? Painting the chairs in the kitchen gave them a new lease of life, for very little cost, and the owner had previously intended to throw them out!

## Techniques

We have chosen two or three of the techniques used in each room, and explained what materials you need, and in clear step-by-steps, exactly how you can achieve the same results. Some of the techniques are used in more than one room.

## In a weekend?

All the rooms that appear in the series were done in two days, and we didn't cheat! Granted, we had some expert help, but we also had films to make, so it is possible! We suggest you rope in a few friends to help – this will help speed up the process, and will make it much more fun – and you can always offer to return the favour, or simply bribe them with plenty of pizza and wine!

All the decorating techniques used in the rooms are easy – as long as you know how! This effect (*right*) was used on the fireplace in the dining room.

## Getting started

**1** Start by listing what you want
from your room. Who is going to
use it, why and when? You could
make a rough plan, or just jot down
your ideas. You could make a sample
board, using fabrics, paint samples
and pictures cut out from magazines.
All our interior designers start by doing
this, and it really helps to focus your
ideas, and to get a good idea of what
will work. You could try painting the
inside of a large box to see how your
colours work together.

**2** Choose a suitable weekend.
This might sound very obvious,
but it's not just a case of making sure
you haven't invited the in-laws to stay.
Will you have to turn the radiators off?
Will you be making lots of noise –
could you choose a weekend when
the neighbours are away? It might be
worth choosing a summer day so that
you can move furniture outside, to
give you plenty of room for
manoeuvre. It might also be a good
idea to get rid of any children and
pets for the weekend. They won't like
the paint fumes, and will probably get
very bored while you are busy.

**3** Be realistic. Assess whether
you are going to need some
professional help from an
electrician or plumber, and book
them well in advance, especially if
you want them at the weekend.
Rather than spending a fortune on
equipment, can you hire or borrow
anything? Or could you arrange to
share equipment with a like-minded
friend? Don't be too ambitious –
begin with a small room so you can
start to gauge how long tasks take.

Stewart Walton
organising the
team (*left*).

We erected a
temporary shelter
so we could work
outside whatever
the weather
(*right*).

Clear your room
completely or
cover the
furniture (*right*) ...

... and cover
yourselves!
(*above*).

Anyone can lend
a hand! (*above*).

## Preparation

1 Clear as much out of the room as you can. Anything that you don't want to move out from the room, move to the centre, and cover with large dust sheets.

2 Wear clothes that you don't mind getting covered in paint. Also, try to avoid wearing wool clothes that might shed onto the paintwork.

3 Prepare your walls. If your walls are painted, wash them thoroughly to remove any grime or grease that might prevent the paint from drying.

Flaky, old paint needs to be scraped and sanded off. Fill in any cracks and other imperfections with plaster filler.

If your walls are papered, you could try painting right over them. As long as the wallpaper is in good condition, this works really well. Alternatively, hire a wallpaper stripper, and start from scratch.

4 Prepare your woodwork. Clean any painted woodwork with a solution of warm soapy water or sugar soap. Any bare patches of wood will need to be painted with a suitable wood primer before painting.

## Equipment

*Paint brushes*
It's worth paying a little bit more for good quality brushes, as they are easier to use and create a good finish. A good brush is shaped at the end to form a wedge shape. This holds the paint well and helps to apply it where you want it. Before dipping a new

Preparation is boring, but essential for good results (*above*).

You can hire equipment such as ladders at local DIY stores (*above*).

brush in a tin of paint, flick the bristles backwards and forwards a few times to get rid of any dust and loose bristles.

For most walls and ceilings use a 10cm/4in or 12cm/5in brush. For smaller areas such as coving, edges and skirting boards, it is more practical to use 2.5 cm/1in brushes.

*Rollers*
Rollers are brilliant for covering large areas such as walls and ceilings in double-quick time. There are several types available, but the best type to use for applying matt emulsion is a sheepskin roller. Use a short-pile one for even surfaces, and a long-pile one for textured or uneven surfaces, such as Artex or over wallpaper.

*Paint*
The range of paints available today can be overwhelming. There are numerous paints for every surface, and in every colour. We have mentioned the type of paint and colour in each project, and listed the actual brand number in the stockists list, where available. The most common type of paint used is vinyl matt emulsion for walls, and a gloss paint for internal woodwork. It is easy to find paints that will create special paint finishes, but it is possible to make your own, which is covered in the technique boxes.

## Tidying up

1 If you have been using water-based paints, rinse your rollers and brushes in cold water, and then wash thoroughly in warm, soapy water. Oil-based paint should be cleaned off using white spirit, and then rinsed with warm, soapy water. Leave your rollers and brushes to dry thoroughly before putting them away. Brushes should be stored flat, and rollers standing up on their handles.

2 If you want to dispose of paint, find out the best way from your local authority. Most will want you to take it to the local dump for special disposal. Never throw paint down the drain. You can throw away empty paint cans in the dustbin.

3 If you get paint on your carpet, or any other surface where you don't want it, clear it up immediately so it doesn't have time to dry. Use warm, soapy water for water-based paints and white spirit for oil-based paints. You will need to rinse this off immediately.

# HALL

PYKE

# W A Y

**F**irst impressions count, and as the hallway is the first room you see when you enter a house, it's worth making it welcoming. Hallways are often narrow, poorly lit places, stuffed full with coats, shoes and other clutter, but with a bit of thought, all this can be overcome!

**Chris and Sarah Stoneham**

'We started to decorate our hallway, but didn't get very far! It would be nice to see some of the original features restored, and to cheer the place up a bit.'

**Jocasta Innes**

'This is an absolutely standard turn-of-the-century, terraced house hallway – complete with all the usual problems. I wanted to add some colour and light, and to restore some of the original features.'

First impressions count and the first impression as we entered Chris and Sarah's house was definitely not a favourable one. The hallway had potential, being very tall, but it was narrow and poorly lit, with dark, oppressive stripped-pine doors. It also appeared as though the family had started decorating and then given up, which, funnily enough, is exactly what had happened.

Chris and Sarah couldn't stand the suffocating purple and pink shag carpet that they had inherited with the house, and they felt the front door was a bit plain. They wanted a cheerful, welcoming, bright hallway, but it also needed to be practical. Chris was keen on having a shelf to put keys and letters on and they needed somewhere to hang up coats. They were also eager to have the original features restored.

**The basics**

Once we'd banished the family from the house it was time to get to work and I felt as though we would need an army to get everything done. The first task was to drop the dado rail to hip height and to move the radiator along. Moving the dado rail instantly restored the correct proportions of the room, and helped to create a feeling of space. Then it was time for the preparation – stripping the paint off the banisters with paint stripper, cleaning down the walls, and filling cracks before priming.

**The colours**

As I couldn't find the colour I wanted for the walls I decided to mix my own using emulsion. I painted broad,

The hallway was tall, narrow and poorly lit. Sarah and Chris wanted to make it bright and welcoming (*right*).

Gluing a large mirror to the wall greatly increased the feeling of space (*below right*).

We were thrilled to find original encaustic tiles under the carpet (*below*).

## Paint spattering

This is so easy that even a beginner can get great results.

- newspaper • base coat • selection of emulsion paints
- long-handled brush
- piece of wood

**1** Spread out plenty of newspaper to protect your floor, then paint the background coat.

**2** Thin down the paint to be used for spattering using tap water.

**3** Dip the brush in the paint then

flick at the wall. Tapping the brush against a piece of wood is very effective. If you find you are getting a blobby effect, add more water to your paint.

**4** Allow each colour to dry before spattering with further colours.

vertical stripes using apricot and cinnamon colour-washes above the dado rail, then went for a pale blue, in a paint spatter effect underneath. Strangely enough, this combination can make a room look wider.

To get beautiful, even stripes, I used a plumb line to mark off vertical lines. I sealed off the areas I didn't want to paint with masses of masking tape, which I peeled off very carefully later.

The spattering effect (see box) is an old Swedish technique. The main thing is to get the paint consistency right; water your paint down so it's thin enough to flick, but not so it dribbles down the wall. Experiment, and water down gradually until you get the consistency right. Two to three shades of one colour look great.

A sloping board down the side of the staircase was perfect for coat hooks (*above*).

The stairs were given a lift with the addition of a blue dugget runner (*left*).

## The mirror

To open the place out and make it lighter we added a huge mirror in a grid frame, which was specially designed to fill the entire wall between the dado rail and the cornice. The obvious place to put it was over a shelf we'd built to go above the radiator. Putting up the shelf was simple, but the mirror proved more problematic. I decided to glue it up, which was possibly more difficult than hanging as it had to be completely flush against the wall and fit like a glove. The end result was well worth all the effort, however, as the mirror really increased the sense of space and added a new mysterious dimension to the narrow hallway.

If you are planning on putting up a mirror, choose one that's safety-backed. Alternatively, rub down the back of the mirror and paint with matt emulsion paint and leave to dry for at least 16 hours before applying any adhesive. When you come to glue the mirror to the wall, ensure that the wall is smooth and that the mirror fits flush against it. You will need to supply a support (a simple shelf, for example) for the mirror to rest on while the glue dries.

## The doors

The front door really needed a lift so we removed the ripple glass that was there and reglazed it with a plain panel. I felt that the door would look wonderful if we painted an imitation stained glass window onto the plain glass using fake leading (which comes in an easy-to-use squeezy tube). This is not as difficult as it sounds as it basically involves tracing around a pre-traced design you've already selected, as opposed to painting freehand.

The first step is to find a design to copy. Copy the design using tracing paper, then stick this to the back of the glass panel. Working on the other side of the panel, trace over the lines with fake leading to transfer the design onto the glass. This takes a while to set so we left Sarah and Chris to colour in the design with glass paints to complete the stained glass effect. The finished panel gives privacy as well as a cheerful welcome to the home.

We painted the internal doors a creamy emulsion to make them less obtrusive, then I crackle-glazed the panels (see box). This created an instant ageing effect which looked very interesting – like crocodile skin.

## The floor and stairs

I was so thrilled when we peeled back the horrid carpet to reveal the original encaustic tiles. All that was needed was to scrape off the odd bit of cement, wash down the tiles, then cover them with floor polish (applied with a roller for speed). After that it was simply a question of giving them a good buff up with a floor cloth. The results were tremendous.

We added a pineapple finial to the newel post, which serves as a visual full-stop (*right*).

The stairs needed a new carpet, so I picked a handsome, rich blue dugget to fit in with the rest of the colour scheme. I left Sarah and Chris to decide if they wanted to take up the underneath pink carpet.

### The finishing touches

We painted the banisters a creamy white, then stained and polished the handrail to make it really glow. To complete the staircase, I added a pineapple finial to the newel post, which gave it back its importance as a visual 'full stop'.

Pictures really help to make a place look welcoming, so we collected some architectural prints and put them in frames which we'd marbled. I'm sure Sarah and Chris will follow up this idea with a print collection of their own.

As it was a hallway, coat hooks were vital. In this case we screwed them onto a sloping board which followed the line of the staircase. Finally, we softened the pendant lights with cheap paper lanterns, then, to really finish things off, we placed a vase of fresh flowers, on top of the newly erected shelf.

## Crackle glazing

- crackle glaze • two water-based paints in contrasting colours • paint brushes • oil-based matt varnish • varnishing brush • hair dryer (optional)

1 Paint on your base coat and leave to dry.

2 Brush over the crackle-glaze base in one direction and allow to dry

3 Paint your second choice of colour on top of the glaze. This will activate the crackle glaze and create the crackle effect. The thicker this top coat, the wider the cracks will be.

4 Leave to dry naturally or use a hair dryer if you want to make the cracks bigger.

5 Finally, varnish the entire area to protect the crackle-glaze finish.

Adding a stained-glass effect to the front door was easier than you might have thought (*left*).

We added architectural prints to the walls (*right*).

*Chris Stoneham*
'We were completely
stunned by the
transformation!
We are very pleased,
especially with the
small shelf and coat
hooks, which will
definitely be useful.'

LOUN

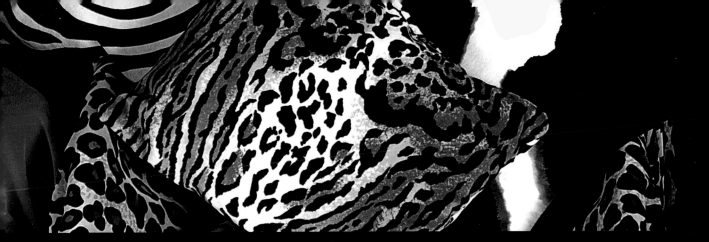

# G E

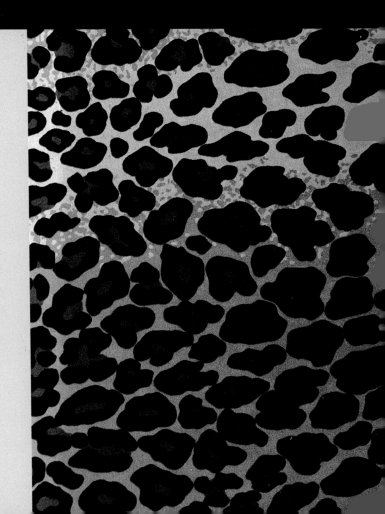

**W**hether you call it a lounge, a sitting room, a living room or a front room, this room is the focus of the house. It's where we spend most of our time (when we're not asleep!), so we need to be happy with the way it looks. It also has to suit the way you live, and suit what you are going to use it for. The four young men who approached us wanted a party room...

*Tom, Ed,
Doc and Jan*

'We're renting this house, so there's no point in us spending a lot of money. But our lounge definitely needs something doing to it. We've warned the landlord, and he's happy about this, but he's going to come and see what you do!'

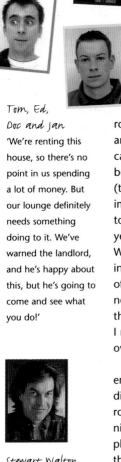

*Stewart Walton*

'This room needs serious help! If we can get past the beer cans and mouldy cheesecake, we're in with a chance. We're not just decorating this room – we're saving their souls!'

In Victorian times the lounge or drawing room was sumptuously furnished to reflect the wealth and status of its owners. Often decorated with a feminine touch, it was reserved for civilised entertaining. In the 1990s, however, things are rather different, especially when the room is being lived in by four young men.

As soon as I walked into this room I was struck by the complete and utter mess – endless empty lager cans, a cabinet full of empty whisky bottles, piles of magazines and videos (the grown-up sort), and a most impressive lump of cheesecake stuck to the wall – a relic from a party a year or two back. And the furniture! Well, let's just say it wasn't exactly inviting. There was definitely no sign of the gentle arts here. Forget crochet, needlepoint and embroidery. In fact, the room was in such a state that I realised that before it could be made over it would have to be mucked out.

Once the room was clean and empty, I sat down with the boys to discuss what they wanted from the room. Primarily, they saw it as a night-time room, which would be a place for entertainment and where they could crash out when they came in from work. They also needed a place where assorted friends could sleep over – presumably when all of the 'entertainment' became too much for them. It had to be a room where there was a 'top shelf' for their library collection and, most importantly, a bar – after all they were hardly going to be sipping afternoon tea in there.

Rich, warm colours and fabrics were called for, with heavy, velvet drapes to

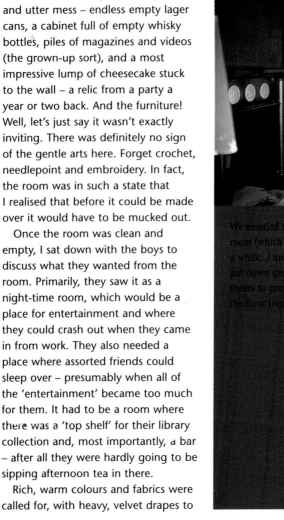

One wall was packed with "top-shelf" videos and books (*right*).

The room was large with high ceilings and a huge window. It had plenty of potential (*left*).

We used a sumptuous green velvet for the curtains, and more velvet for the throws (*right*).

We emptied the room (which took a while...) and put down ground sheets to protect the floor (*right*).

26

ensure privacy (we wouldn't want
to shock the neighbours), and an
abundance of covers and throws so
they could lounge about in comfort.
What the boys needed was a bar-cum-
games-room-cum-library-cum-
occasional bedroom, which would be
a place to drink, play and chill out.
In other words, they wanted an old-
fashioned gentleman's club room.

### The colours

Having already decided that rich,
warm, Victorian-style colours were
appropriate, I chose a palette of
deliciously edible reds and browns.
We painted the walls using dark
orange emulsion, followed by a colour
wash of tomato-ketchup red.

I also used this red on the door and
window frames as a unifying element,
while the ceiling, shelves, bar and
skirting board were painted with a
very Victorian shade of brown.
However, when it came to the
beautiful and ornate cornice nothing
but gold would do.

The mantelpiece was already
wonderfully dramatic with its columns
and round marble insets. However,
when we turned up it was painted
white which made it look rather bland.
This was a grand feature and deserved
a bit of drama, so I cleaned up the
round marble inserts, painted the rest
black and picked out the wonderful
columns with gold paint to match the
ceiling cornice.

## Making silhouettes

- camera and film
- scalpel or small,
sharp scissors
- permanent black
marker pen • PVA
glue • cardboard
- ready-made photo frame

**1** Photograph your
subject in profile
against a white
background.

**2** Carefully cut
around the
profile using a scalpel
or scissors.

**3** Colour in the
back of the
image with black
marker pen.

**4** Carefully glue
your silhouette
onto cardboard, and
then put in the frame.

The finished bar stocked with bottles of whisky (*left*).

When we turned up there were two medals hanging on the wall. They looked rather lost, so we gave them this grand, imperial setting (*right*), which ties in with the gentlemen's club room theme.

## The furniture

The room already had a cabinet, filled with whisky bottles, but I thought we could do a bit better than that. I had no doubt that the bar would be the main attraction of the room, so I felt that we shouldn't hold back. We could work with the existing shelves, but we wanted to build a fridge into the bar and dress it all up a bit.

The animal print upholstered bar stools lent a touch of 1950s Soho to the scene, which was particularly appropriate considering the bar was going to be so well stocked, it could grace a nightclub. The stools were simple to upholster: we placed a circle of foam on top of the seat, topped it with a circle of wadding, then finally with a circle of animal print fabric. The whole lot was secured with a staple gun, which is an interior decorator's favourite gadget!

To make the chairs and sofas more inviting, we simply covered them with throws and added piles of cushions. It is amazing how a tired piece of furniture can be transformed with a piece of material thrown over it and tucked in at the corners, and it's a great deal cheaper and easier than getting it completely re-upholstered. We jazzed up the cushion fabrics using bleach and a stamping technique that uses bronzing powder (see box). We opted for simple stars and fleur-de-lys.

## The fabrics

What could be more appropriate for a gentleman's club room than velvet? And when we teamed it with fake, furry animal print cushions, the effect was wonderfully louche - a touch of colonial decadence.

I chose dark green, lovely, silky velvet for the full length curtains and, continuing with the Victorian theme, used heavy swags of the same material draped to make a pelmet.

## The finishing touches

The walls were looking a bit bare so for a bit of fun, I stuck some animal print fabric on to carpet underlay and cut it out in a rough, human shape, then hung it on the wall – these boys take no prisoners.

For a bit of extra interest I decided to decorate the walls with silhouettes, and I gave them an extra twist by personalising them (see box) and setting them in frames within frames. We also added coats of arms, which are just children's plastic toys, spray-painted white, and which add a nice touch of frivolity.

The group of chunky church candles on the mantelpiece look dramatic and will add to the atmosphere when lit.

## The practical side

I addressed the issue of friends sleeping over by hiding futons inside large cushion covers.

Considering the 'adult' content of most of the books and videos, no ordinary shelf or bracket would do, so I devised a style I christened 'muscular Gothic' (inspired by the great Victorian designer, Charles Eastlake). We made new brackets from MDF, and sprayed them silver, making them look like Spice Girls' knickers.

The finished room was a mix of traditional and modern (*opposite page*).

Animal-print human shapes added wildman decor to the plain walls (*left*).

Nothing but gold paint would do for this beautiful, elaborate cornice (*below*).

### Bleaching cushions

• **sheet of cardboard** • **scalpel** • **small brush** • **household bleach**

1 Cut the shape you want out of cardboard using a scalpel to make a stencil. We used stars and heraldry symbols.

2 Place the sheet of cardboard with the cut out design onto the chosen material, then using a brush apply household bleach evenly onto the material through the stencil.

3 Allow to dry, then wash the material to get rid of the smell and to prevent the bleach rotting it.

### Stamping material with bronzing powder

• PVA or any water-based glue
• rubber stamp • bronzing powder
• soft artist's brush

1 Apply glue to your stamp, avoiding the recesses.

2 Press onto the material, making sure that plenty of glue transfers to the fabric. Repeat all over your material.

3 Using a brush, sprinkle the bronzing powder over the fabric. It may help to tap your brush lightly.

4 Shake off any excess powder. Leave to dry.

Tom, Ed, Doc
and Jan
'It's excellent – and
we particularly like
the bar! You've
thought of
everything, and it
looks fantastic.
Thanks Stewart and
the decorating team!'

# KITCH

# E N

**K**itchens are probably
the most difficult
rooms to transform.
Modern, fitted kitchens are
often soulless, mass-produced
affairs, which date quickly,
and it can be a real challenge
to make them look better –
especially in just a weekend!
It can cost a fortune to replace
kitchen units and equipment,
and we found a more cost-
effective solution.

**Philomena Beggs**
'I knew Bernadette had tried to come up with a colour scheme and failed. She copied her current scheme, yellow, from a brochure. She likes her fish and hates the tables and chairs she inherited when she bought the flat. She would like a completely new kitchen, but can't afford it.'

**Catherine Woram**
'Bernadette had painted her kitchen yellow because it seemed an easy choice. She now wants something that is more colourful, but still easy to live with.'

Philomena and her daughter Ursula were housesitting for Bernadette for the weekend. She often goes away, but this time they thought they'd surprise her while she was away. The kitchen wasn't in bad condition, but they knew Bernadette was bored with it, and fancied a new colour. She also hated the carpet, so we started by throwing it out. The kitchen was large, with good storage, so we had plenty to work with.

## The walls

A built-in fish tank is the focal point of the room and I suggested orange for the colour of the walls, to complement the colour of the goldfish! We put the goldfish in a bucket for the weekend, and got to work. When the orange paint was dry, we decided to add stencilled words to give a bit of interest to the walls. I chose cream paint for the 'fishy' words which offered a contrast, without the obvious harshness of white. (The woodwork and part of the floor was also painted in cream, though in an oil-based version of the paint.) I used letters cut out from a newspaper and enlarged them on a photocopier to the size I wanted. I then stuck them onto a sheet of acetate using spray mount, and carefully cut round the letter using a sharp knife to make a stencil out of the acetate. To make sure all the letters lined up on the wall, we stuck a line of masking tape on the wall where we wanted the words to go, and then stuck the letter stencils above it, again using masking tape. We dabbed on cream emulsion using a stencil brush. We used the same method on the radiator, but it was a little trickier as it was an uneven surface.

The built-in kitchen was starting to look dated and boring (*left*). We decided to replace the cupboard doors (*below*).

The large windows offer good, natural light (*right*).

The focal point of the room is this built-in fish tank (*left*).

## The floor

We decided to sand the floorboards, and to paint them. Painting your floorboards is a great, inexpensive way to change the look of a floor. As all you need is paint, varnish, and the hire of a sander for the day, it is cheaper even than lino tiles. It doesn't matter if the boards are marked or an uneven colour, as the paint covers all manner of sins. I decided to paint a blue and cream chequerboard effect, to co-ordinate with the wall tiles. It is much simpler than you might think (see box). One handy tip though – be sure to wear knee pads as this task will involve hours spent on your knees.

## The table

Bernadette was planning to throw out her kitchen table and chairs because they were a very boring, varnished pine. But we thought we'd give them a new lease of life first, and see if she wanted to keep them once she'd seen their transformation. The idea was to give them a rustic feel, so we started by stripping the varnish off the table with a belt sander. We then applied a primer solution for 10 minutes, followed by a wood bleach, which we left on for 3-4 hours. You can buy products that will do this for you – just ask in a DIY store. We had to sand the chairs by hand, which took ages, but was worth it.

The new kitchen doors are very simple, which suits the modern look we were trying to create.

There are hundreds of attractive, inexpensive kitchen accessories available, and they can instantly update your room (*right*).

## The kitchen units

Rather than rip out all the units, we decided to change the cupboard doors. You can buy new fronts for cabinets, but these come in a limited range of designs and sizes, and usually cost a fortune, so we opted to make our own. You might be surprised to hear that this is actually a much cheaper and easier option than buying complete, new doors, so it is worth thinking about.

We removed the existing cupboard doors and drew round them on paper to make templates. We took the templates to a local DIY store, where they were happy to cut the wood to the sizes we needed for no charge. They were happy to do this because we were buying their wood. You will probably need to sand the edges, but getting the doors cut professionally takes an element of risk out of the job – and saves lots of time.

We painted the doors with emulsion as a base coat. We then sponged on smoke-coloured paint, which was watered down, to give a distressed, 'country' look. When dry, the doors were sealed with varnish to give a tough surface. As the doors had been so inexpensive, we added new handles to complete the look. We then simply reused the hinges from the previous doors to attach the new doors to the old cabinets.

We replaced the existing Formica worktop with beechwood.

There was an ugly boiler in the corner of the dining area, which we disguised by constructing a cupboard, made to echo the style of the main door to the kitchen. There was room for a couple of shelves and we added the same style of handles that we'd already used for the kitchen cabinets.

The finished kitchen looks brighter, warmer and more welcoming (*opposite*).

We chose brightly coloured mugs to co-ordinate with the room (*right*).

The chairs were given a new lease of life, and were saved from the scrap heap (*left*).

## Painting a wood floor

• industrial sanding machine • cream vinyl matt emulsion paint • blue vinyl matt emulsion paint • 2 cork floor tiles (30cm/12in square) • pencil for tracing • 1 fine paintbrush for edges • masking tape • 5cm/2in paintbrush to fill in the squares • 10cm/4in paintbrush for base colour • Dead Flat decorator's varnish to seal the colour

1 Sand the boards using a sanding machine, and sweep well to remove any traces of sawdust.

2 Apply two coats of cream emulsion paint using the largest brush, allowing to dry between coats.

3 Using a pencil, and working from one corner of the room, mark out the squares, using the floor tile as a template. Marking them diagonally to the floorboards, in diamonds, creates an illusion of space.

4 Using the fine paint brush, paint the edges of each alternate square with the blue emulsion paint. You can put masking tape around the squares if you like. Fill in every other square using the 5cm/2in brush.

5 When the floor is completely dry, apply 2-3 coats of Dead Flat varnish, allowing to dry completely between each coat.

Bernadette already had an attractive mirror which suited the room perfectly (*left*).

We painted the tiles above the cooker to match the floor (*right*).

### The tiles

Rather than replacing the tile splash-back, we decided to paint the existing tiles. After making sure the tiles were completely clean, we painted on one coat of tile primer. When dry, we painted the tiles using a gloss version of the blue and cream colours used on the floor. We used a small roller brush, such as one you might use for painting a stamp, to get a smoother finish than if using a regular paintbrush.

### The door

The existing back door had unattractive, textured glass panes, one of which had been replaced in the past, and now didn't match. I used a terracotta-coloured glass paint to paint alternate panes of glass, which added interest, and echoed the chequered design of the floor and tiles.

### The finishing touches

We had planned to put a 'lazy Sheila' on the ceiling, which is a rack for

## Distressing paintwork

- **2 colours of emulsion paint** • **wax candle** • **medium grade wire wool** • **5cm/2in paintbrush** • **10cm/4in paintbrush** • **acrylic matt varnish**

**1** Paint the cupboard doors using the paint you want as a base. This normally works best if it is the lighter colour.

**2** Dilute your second paint colour, 3 parts water to 1 part paint. Apply an even coat over your painted surface. It will not form an even cover, and your original colour will show through.

**3** Once dry, rub a household candle over the paintwork, using quite a firm pressure, then brush off any loose wax.

**4** Apply a second coat of your paint/water mixture, and allow it to dry. You could use a contrasting colour for the second coat, but keeping the same colour creates a more subtle effect.

**5** When this is dry, use the wire wool to rub over the entire surface of the paint. This achieves the distressed look.

**6** Finally varnish the whole surface of each cupboard door to protect the paintwork – and to make them easier to clean.

hanging pots, pans and utensils, but it proved a little trickier than expected. We needed to find a joist to attach it to, and the only way to do this is to drill holes in the ceiling until you find it. But there wasn't one, and we were left with lots of little drill holes! So, we got out the polyfiller and paint, and repaired the damage! We put up a very nice wall rack instead! Bernadette already had a very attractive mirror, which went very well with the new colour scheme.

*Bernadette McDermott*

'I love the colours. I would never have thought to paint the kitchen such bright colours. The floor looks amazing – painting it is a really clever, cheap way of transforming it and matching it to the painted tiles brings the whole room together. My fish are pleased with their wall, but I think it's good they can't read...'

Rioja Bordeaux
Muscadet Chianti

# DINING

# ROOM

**W**ith today's busy lives, it is getting harder to find time to sit down and enjoy a meal as a family. But when it does happen, it is fun to make it an occasion, and we wanted to create a dining room that provided a dramatic setting. If you don't have a separate dining room, candles and unusual lighting can help to change a day room into something more interesting.

*Irene and Eric Thomson*

'We would like a dining room where we have room for all our family to eat. We'd also quite like a separate table for the children.'

*Marta Nowicka*

'I wanted to unify the space and create a strong, dramatic dining experience, with surreal, simple yet abstract, functional forms.'

Irene and Eric Thomson live in a big, rambling house in Bude, north Cornwall. Used as a hotel in the 1920s, their house is set in a beautiful location overlooking the sea. Irene and Eric wanted to make their large dining room more interesting and welcoming, especially as they like to have large family and friends get-togethers. They have four children, Sally (16), Jill (15), Lorna (11) and Craig (4), so need plenty of space.

The Thomson's dining room is large, light and airy, and has the most beautiful bay window, but the room needed a new lease of life. The family had bought a beautiful chandelier, but had otherwise not touched the room for many years. When I spoke to the family they told me that they can have up to 8 adults and 6 kids dining on occasion, and the room needed to have space for all these people to be seated comfortably. Irene and Eric ideally wanted a separate eating area for the children.

One of the most striking features of the room was the fireplace, which Irene said they didn't use when they were eating in there, because people burnt their backs! It seemed a shame, and we were all keen to try and solve this problem.

### The inspiration

When I was out on the beach, I found a wonderful, white, chalk stone with a hole right through it. This was the inspiration for the tables, and using the curved shape helped to break up the rectangular form of the room. We even cut oval holes out of the tables. I decided to continue the sea concept by painting the walls deep, dark blue. We used white for all the other features in the room.

The furniture in the room needed updating and making more comfortable (*right*), so we decided to cover the chairs and add cushions.

The Thomson's dining room was large, with plenty of potential, but it was absolutely jam-packed with furniture (*left*).

We replaced the dining table with two intersecting tables made from MDF (*right*).

This pretty, arch-shaped window became more prominent framed by the dark blue wall colour (*left*).

## The planning

The planning of this rectangular dining room posed a challenge as it featured a large bay window area, creating two distinct spaces which intersected one another. The challenge was to unify the whole room with no dead space. The bay window is very deep, so I decided to use the bay window as a seating area for the children. By adding a smaller version of the main table to this area, the room became a more unified whole.

The floor was in such good condition that we were happy to leave the beauty of the wood to shine through. There was one white-painted floorboard by the fireplace, which we painted the same blue as the walls. We then addressed the windows.

The room has three beautiful windows: one large bay window overlooking the sea (about 4ft deep, and 6ft wide, narrowing to 2ft at the front), a smaller window next to the fireplace and an arch-shaped window above the piano. Irene and Eric took down the curtains before we arrived, as they really didn't like them. We also removed the pelmets.

47

The finished dining room: very simple, but very effective (*left*).

This wonderful, white, chalk stone was the inspiration behind the table design (*bottom*).

## The fireplace surround

We cut our MDF using a jigsaw, but you could ask in your local DIY store if they will cut it for you. Many will do this for you for free, or for a small charge if you buy the MDF from them.

• jigsaw • **MDF** • **sandpaper** • **pencil** • **mastic gun and silicon mastic** • **vinyl matt emulsion paint** • **varnish**

1 Cut your MDF to the size required using a jigsaw, or get your local DIY store to do it for you. Sand all the edges.

2 Lightly pencil your design on the MDF. We chose wine names.

3 Carefully pipe the mastic over your pencilling of the the words. At the end of each word, quickly pull the mastic away from the board to cut the flow of mastic, and to give a soft and neat finish to the writing.

4 Leave the words for 2-3 hours. The mastic will not set hard.

5 Carefully apply paint over the entire board with your chosen paint. Be sure to get the paint underneath and in

6 When the paint is dry, varnish the whole surround to protect the paintwork and your mastic letters.

between each letter to make sure that you don't have any white surfaces showing.

## The dining tables

Although the Thomsons already had a large, attractive table, it wasn't big enough to seat everyone at large, family gatherings. We thought it would be fun to start again, using the oval shape of the stone for inspiration.

We built the two dining tables from MDF. We cut out our shapes using a jigsaw, but you might like to ask your local DIY store if they will do this for you. We painted the tables using white emulsion. The tables are set on castors and are designed to fit together, with one slightly higher than the other. I thought having two tables would give flexibility, depending on the amount of people dining at any one time. They could be joined for one large dinner party, and when separated,

would provide one table for the children, with a separate one for the adults.

## The lights

The room already had two wall lamps either side of the bay window, which we decided to update. There was a plaster rose on the ceiling that had an ugly hanging light which we were all keen to change.

## Fabric wall hangings

My lack of patience with intricate things such as sewing means that I always use double-sided sticky tape, velcro and staple guns wherever possible! I used velcro to fasten these wall hangings, which makes them easily removable for washing.

• tape measure fabric (we used white butter muslin) • bonding web • white velcro • staple gun

1 Measure the wall area you wish to cover. This will give you the length required for your wall hanging.

2 Cut your fabric to the length required. You don't need to trim the width of the fabric – simply keep to the original width. Allow 5cm/2in at both the top and bottom for hems. This will protect the fabric from fraying, and provide a neat edge.

3 Hem the edges using iron-on

bondaweb. Simply position the strip of bondaweb 2.5cm/1in from the edge of the fabric, fold over the fabric and iron to fasten. Repeat on all edges. Iron all your wall hangings using a low heat setting.

4 Sew one part of the velcro strips to the top edge of your fabric. Staple the other to the top of your picture rail.

5 Fasten the fabric to the ledge. The wall hangings can be removed easily for washing.

We removed all the lighting already in the room, along with the fittings. We then hired an electrician to add some amazing cord lights, which he threaded through the ceiling – this is definitely not a job for the DIY novice! We moved the 'octopus' chandelier towards the piano area, which was essentially a 'dead' corner of the room, to create brightness and interest.

We brought in lots of white candles of varying thicknesses and heights. Candles are essential for evening dining – they really add to the atmosphere, and they are often very inexpensive. We positioned our candles directly onto the table, which looked very striking. The melted wax is easily removed from the MDF surface, but if you prefer, candle holders are easily found. Something simple such as wrought iron would work well.

### The fireplace

The fireplace is oak with a brick panel inside this. Irene had started to sand the wood, but she thought it could do with more to really bring the grain out. The brickwork had been painted with red gloss paint before the Thomsons moved in, and Irene had started to remove this also. There are two dragons and two cherubs carved into it. We thought about restoring the fireplace, but that would not have solved the problem of burning the backs of the guests!

We decided to add an MDF cover, which would modernise the fireplace, and protect the guests. We cut this to fit, and then wrote on the names of wines in sealant mastic. Irene and Eric are wine fans (aren't we all?), so we thought they would enjoy this touch. When dry, we painted over the whole cover, to give a raised effect, which

reflected the raised texture of the walls (see box). We added a light behind the cover, which created a glow around the fireplace area. This added atmosphere, without the threat of overheating the guests. The cover and light could be removed if the family ever wanted to use the real fire.

### The walls and ceiling

The walls below the dado rail were papered with a raised-pattern wallpaper, and the walls above with a plain, flat paper. If your wallpaper is in good condition, it is worth simply painting over it. There is no need to strip the walls. As old houses often have uneven walls, you often have to repaper with lining paper. Painting over existing wallpaper saves you the trouble!

To even out the two surfaces I applied textured wallpaper polyfiller to the walls. The surface remained uneven – it would be impossible to completely smooth out the surface, but we did manage to make the room more unified. The walls were painted with blue emulsion and panels of muslin were hung from the picture rail, again to conceal the wallpaper texture and to soften the atmosphere in the room (see box). The ceiling and all the woodwork in the room was painted in pure, brilliant white.

### The finishing touches

We added pillows with white pillow cases to the window sill for seats, and tied white pillow cases around the dining chairs. Simple, white lilies were added to the table. We also found some very simple plates and glassware. Finally, we covered the stereo speakers with fishing nets to soften them, and to tie in with the sea concept.

Irene and Eric
Thomson
'We were completely
amazed. The tables
are very unusual, and
we love the fireplace.'

# MUSIC

# ROOM

**F**ew of us have space for a dedicated music room, but the O'Connors have musical sons, and wanted somewhere for them to practise and perform. David Carter's striking design shows what you can achieve if you let your imagination run riot with a theme.

*Pat and Wendy*
*O'Connor*
'When we moved
here we hoped that
we'd be able to make
this into a music
room for our two
sons. We've had
Uncle Bob a little
while and would
like to keep him.'

*David Carter*
'I'd normally describe
my job as a labour of
love, however this job
came closer to a one-
night stand.'

**M**usic rooms are not rooms that most people would think of having – you certainly do not see them on most estate agents' details. Yet for an interior decorator they present a wonderful opportunity to create a room that exists simply to stimulate and satisfy the senses.

Prior to this I had only done one music room, yet that must rank as one of my favourites. 'A harem for the soul' was how my clients described it. The scheme I devised for Wendy and Pat was based loosely on this previous one, although time constraints meant that it had to be simplified. They did not have any major requests, other than we keep Uncle Bob – an automaton who had obviously become one of the family.

As this was going to be a music room I felt it needed a touch of drama, something flamboyant, yet not over the top. This was a place for performances, a stage if you like. As so many musical instruments are such wonderful shapes, I decided to use these as the basis for the scheme. I decided on giant violins for the walls and french horns for the fireplace.

**The preparation**
The first thing to do with any room is to strip it down to an empty shell – removing carpets, furniture, pictures etc. Once the room is completely bare, and stripped of all potential distractions, it is easier to get an idea of its potential. It becomes a blank canvas, primed and ready for new colours and shapes.

I'd normally describe my work as a labour of love, however, this job came closer to a one-night stand. The problem was that we had to compress

The O'Connors used this room to store furniture, and as a general sitting room. As their sons are musical, they wanted somewhere where they could practise (*left and below*).

We made giant stencils to paint the violins on the walls (*right*).

We painted the fireplace and added a cover. The lily design echoes the shape of the horn (*opposite*).

56

what would typically be several weeks, work into just a couple of days. Simply stripping the wallpaper proved a huge task in itself – what we had thought would be a couple of layers turned out to be seven, and took as many hours to scrape off, even with the help of a heavy-duty steamer.

After we'd removed the wallpaper, we took down the picture rail, then it was time to 'key' the woodwork.

In other words, we gave it a light sand down to create a suitable surface to accept paint. I scoured the room for any holes or cracks which, once detected, were filled, then left to dry before being gently sanded back to a smooth finish.

### The paints and finishes

For a base coat I applied two coats of pink vinyl silk emulsion, then set to

mixing a glaze. For this I used red vinyl matt emulsion, acrylic scumble glaze and water (see box).

I colour-washed the walls by applying the glaze with criss-cross strokes, softening it out with a dry brush and clean rag as I went along. This isn't the sort of job one can stop and start. It has to be done in one go, and at speed, to avoid any messy patches. I applied two coats.

## Silk screen printing

We used this technique on the upholstered chair seats. We chose the silhouette of a musical composer's head, but any bold shape will work just as well.

- **craft knife** • **newspaper** • **fabric (we used 9oz natural cotton duck)** • **large piece of wood or flat surface** • **strong adhesive tape** • **silk screen** • **pigment** • **squeegee** • **iron and ironing board** • **high pressure hose**

**1** Photocopy your design to the size you require and cut it out. Place it on some newspaper and cut around the shape. The outline will be your stencil.

**2** Iron your fabric thoroughly, then secure onto a large piece of wood or flat surface using the strong adhesive tape.

**3** Secure the stencil to the fabric and then lace the silk screen over the top of the stencil. Pour the pigment in a line along the inside of the screen along the edge which is furthest from you. Using the squeegee, pull the pigment slowly across the screen to cover the image.

**4** Carefully lift the screen off the fabric. The stencil may well cling to the screen, however, this can be peeled off easily.

**5** It's a good idea to wash the screen immediately, ideally with a high pressure hose to prevent it from becoming blocked with pigment.

**6** Once the pigment is dry, press the fabric with an iron to fix the dye to the fabric.

### The stencils

To make the stencils, simply find a design you want to copy, or draw your own design, then get it blown up to the size you require at your local photocopying shop. Next, spray mount or paste it onto stencil card. Then, using a craft knife or scalpel, carefully cut around the edge of the design. Remove the cut out and you have your template.

The most tricky bit is calculating the position of the instruments on each wall. It was very important that we got this right, as too many and the design would look crowded, too few and the impact would be lost. I used a pencil and a spirit level to mark up where the top and bottom of the instruments would be. We masked off the borders and applied a charcoal black glaze to the border areas to create a frame. The instruments would have looked odd just floating in space. In a room with a lower ceiling, however, I would suggest using the skirting board and cornice as a framing device.

After working out the position of the instruments on each wall, we came to the fun part – painting the instruments! I used a spray mount fixative on the back of the instrument stencil and stuck it on the wall. We then applied a gold glaze with large brushes, using a scrubbing action to create a textured finish.

When the gold paint had dried, we used another stencil for the fret designs. To create contrast, we used more of the charcoal black paint that we had used for the frame.

### The furniture

As this was a room for performances there had to be somewhere for the audience to sit. We decided that the

We chose a 30s-style design for the dramatic curtains (*top*).

A horn and candles made a dramatic finish to the fireplace (*bottom*).

Uncle Bob looking very comfortable in his top hat and tails (*left*).

## Glazing

- pink vinyl silk emulsion for the base colour, red vinyl matt for the glaze • acrylic scumble glaze • water • brushes • rags
- one dry softening brush

**1** Apply two coats of pink vinyl silk emulsion to the walls as a base. Leave this to dry.

**2** To make a glaze, mix two parts of red vinyl matt emulsion with seven parts of the acrylic scumble glaze and one part water.

**3** Apply the glaze like a colour-wash, with criss-cross strokes, softening out the surface with a dry brush and clean rag as you go. On larger walls it may be easier to divide the work between two people (one can apply the glaze while the other softens out). This is because once the glaze dries out it is no longer possible to manipulate the colours on the wall. You could also use a misting spray.

sweeping to do the room justice and I felt a 30s-inspired design would work well here.

To hide all the bits and pieces which accumulate in any room I designed a tall, cut-out screen – again following the music theme. Next we used two skin-covered drums to act as novel light shades. These threw a lovely diffused light over the room, and looked unusual, without distracting from the other design features.

Naturally the final task was to dress up Uncle Bob – after all, his slightly shabby clothes didn't do justice to such a glamorous room. Under the circumstances, it was obvious, nothing but top hat and tails would do.

old pine chairs would not do as they were, so we decided to give them a face lift.

We started by sanding the chairs and then painted them with red oxide paint. When dry, we painted them with gold paint, then sanded them with wire wool so some of the red would show through the gold. This resulted in a rich, burnished finish. We completed the transformation

of the chairs by covering them with cotton, dyed in the bath with tea bags to create a lovely, warm, golden colour. We then used a silk screen to print on a design of the head of a composer (see box).

### The finishing touches

As the window area was so large the curtains would obviously be a major feature. They really had to be

Pat and Wendy
O'Connor
'It was a great
experience for us, and
especially for our son
James, who now plays
piano in this room.
We are absolutely
delighted with it.'

# BEDR

# Master

# OOM

**B**edrooms can be difficult places to design because you often have to take into account two different tastes! They have to be a place that makes you feel relaxed, so it's a good idea to keep a bedroom as uncluttered as possible. If your clothes, books, toiletries and all the other things we keep in our bedrooms are out of sight, you will have a calm, restful room.

*Shirley and Bill Diamond*

'The room we have as our bedroom at the moment is too small to house our wardrobes, and Bill keeps banging his head when he gets out of bed on the sloping ceiling. We'd like to swap rooms with the kids' playroom as it is much larger and has a wonderful view.'

*Lesley Taylor*

'Shirley and Bill have the most wonderful house, with breathtaking views of the surrounding Welsh countryside. I wanted to create a romantic bedroom for them that made the most of this unique setting.'

**S**hirley Diamond wanted us to transform the room they use as the children's playroom, so we moved out all the games, toys and furniture – the kids then moved into Shirley and Bill's old bedroom. We were left with a very large, simple room, with very little architectural detail, but what makes this room so wonderful is the huge patio windows offering an uninhibited view of the surrounding Welsh countryside. With unrivalled views of the Severn Estuary, this is the best view that the house has, so Shirley and I felt that it was about time this room made the most of this stunning feature.

In design terms, the simplicity of the room meant that, with the exception of creating a furniture layout which made the most of the view, any number of decorative styles could be chosen for the room. The only guideline that Shirley gave me was a request for a touch of romance. Because of the location of the house, I felt it would be apt to choose a Celtic theme for the room, keeping the colours light, soft and romantic.

To add a luxurious feel, I used rich purple and gold, colours inspired by images of past Welsh royalty, discovered during my research around the local area.

**The furniture**

Shirley had two 1960s-style wardrobes, which were very square and fairly uninteresting but, nevertheless, were solid and offered good storage. I felt free-standing furniture was a must in such a setting; built-in furniture would look structured and less romantic, so I decided to revamp these existing pieces. The wardrobes and dressing table were first sanded to remove the

The dark blue carpet and coving darken the room, which is a shame when the room offers so much natural light (*right*).

The transformed wardrobe and dressing table (*right*).

The room was being used as a playroom and general store (*left*).

The rain managed to hold off for a couple of hours, which was useful when we had to work on the wardrobes (*right*).

surface lacquer, and to enable paint to adhere to the surface. We added traditional timber coving to the top of the wardrobes to give height and character, along with simple, panel mouldings which added relief and interest to the doors.

Two coats of ivory-coloured matt emulsion paint were applied. This was followed by the application of a gilding cream to highlight the relief mouldings and cove (see box). The wardrobe door handles were replaced with reproduction gilded ones. We also replaced the hard-edged, oblong mirrors inside the wardrobes with oval mirrors, which looked softer. The final touch was the addition of turned feet.

## Gilding furniture

- sand paper • wood primer • masking tape • vinyl matt emulsion (we used a cream colour) • gold gilding cream
- cloth or small paint brush • button polish

**1** Sand the wardrobe to remove any traces of old varnish and paint. Remove the handles.

**2** Paint the whole wardrobe with wood primer. Once dry, apply two coats of paint.

**3** When dry, mask off the features you want to gild to protect the surrounding areas.

**4** Place a little gilding cream on a dry cloth or paint brush and apply to the selected area.

**5** Once the gilding is dry, rub button polish all over the wardrobe to protect the paint and gild work, and give it a subtle sheen.

The amount of gilding cream used depends on how dramatic a look you want to achieve.

## Fabric stencilling

Making your own stencil gives you the freedom to choose any design you want. Have a look through lots of books and magazines for inspiration – or copy something you already have in your room, such as the wallpaper design. Remember that the motif has to be cut out, so to achieve a good result, try using a bold, simple shape at first and work up to more detailed designs.

- craft knife - waxed stencil card
- spray mount - fabric paint - saucer
- newspaper - small stencilling brush
- thin white fabric (e.g. cotton)

**1** To make a stencil, first photocopy your chosen motif, and enlarge or reduce as required. Secure it to a piece of waxed card with spray mount and cut out the shape using a craft knife.

**2** Attach the stencil to the fabric with spray mount. Only use a little. The glue will lift off with Step 4.

**3** Tip a little fabric paint onto a saucer. Take up a little of the paint onto the tips of the stencil brush and blot onto newspaper. Build up the paint inside the stencil lightly. Try not to get too much paint on the stencil itself; if you do, carefully wipe the stencil. If further colours are being used, repeat on the selected areas.

**4** Cover the stencilled fabric with a thin piece of white fabric, and using a warm iron, carefully press the stencilled fabric. This helps to set the design, and to flatten the fabric.

### The walls and ceiling
After stripping all the wallpaper, and preparing the surfaces, we painted the walls, ceiling and coving with a soft ivory emulsion. This was the final colour on the ceiling and coving, but was used as the base for a colour-washed effect on the walls.

When the walls were dry, a preparatory lemon glaze was applied using a large paint brush. We then mixed two additional beige colours with some extra lemon glaze. These were then sponged onto the walls using large, natural sponges. We blended the three colours with a dragging brush to give a soft, gently blended, romantic effect.

### The carpet
A cream carpet was fitted throughout the room to give the room as large an appearance as possible, and to make the most of the natural light. It also

Ceiling to floor curtains give a luxurious feel to a room. The rich purple silk, combined with the gold and green stencilling adds to the expensive, sumptuous look. We continued the stencil theme onto the muslin curtains (*left*).

Tie-backs are simple to make, and add an attractive finishing touch to curtains. You could try covering your old tiebacks with your new curtain fabric (*left*).

provided a soft, warm background to co-ordinate with the other features in the room.

### The curtains

I chose a rich, royal purple, dressmaking silk for the curtains, and to add weight and body to the curtains, we made them up using cotton bump interlining. This sits between the curtains and lining, adding body and durability. You might

be surprised, but this actually makes a very cost effective curtain fabric. One word of warning though: dressmaking fabrics are not as colour-fast as those fabrics specifically made for curtaining, and can fade.

We added a pair of sheer muslin curtains to the windows for additional protection against the effects of the sun. The main curtains were basic pencil pleat on a curtain runner. To disguise the runner, we added an easy-to-make fabric pelmet suspended from a wrought iron pole. Using lots of layers of fabric creates a fluid, romantic feel. Simply cut a length of fabric 1½ times the width of the window, by ⅛th of the window drop. Hem, and sew on curtain clips approximately 25-30cm/10-12in apart. These clips then hook onto the pole rings. The silk pelmet above the bed was made in the same way as the curtains. The edges of the curtains,

the pelmet hem and the curtain ties have been stencilled using a fabric paint. This was a Celtic knot and disc design that I found. The pelmet above the bed was stencilled with a border of words from an old Welsh poem.

### The bed

We used more purple silk for a bed valance, over which a cream damask bedspread and crisp, white, cotton bedding dressed the bed. The bed was Shirley's own, but the addition of a black, wrought iron headboard gave it a completely new look.

### The final touches

We added a black, iron, pendant light and a free-standing candelabra, which looked very striking with tall, cream candles. We covered the small bedside table with cream damask material, which we cut into a large circle, and hemmed to make a simple table cloth.

*Shirley Diamond*
'It's a good interpretation of the word 'romantic'; I expected it to be more frilly. It's just beautiful. I wouldn't have believed it to be possible to do this in two days... The bedroom is a sheer delight and has given Bill a whole new lease of life!'

# Child's

# OOM

For young people and children, a bedroom isn't just somewhere to sleep. It's the only room in the house they can call their own, so it acts as a den, somewhere to see their friends, and a place to hide from the rest of the family. Let the room owner have their say about the decor – anything for an easy life!

Rachel Pilkington

'I inherited my room from my older sister Naomi – it's dull and girlie. The bed being in the middle of the room is a nuisance and I don't like the wardrobes. I love dancing but I've got nowhere to do it.'

Stewart Walton

'Rachel had a bedroom that had been very well decorated, but it wasn't the bedroom that she wanted, so with the blessing of her parents, we started from scratch.'

**R**achel is 11 years old. She has recently swapped rooms with her older sister Naomi and although the room has been very well decorated, she hates it. The room was decorated with Naomi in mind 18 months ago and they have very different tastes. Respectable and anonymous, the room showed no signs of the youth culture that Rachel felt herself to be part of. The walls were covered in posters, which were there to cover up the decor, not to be a part of it.

A child's bedroom is often the only room where they can express themselves, and it is vital they have a say about what goes in it. There's no point spending a fortune decorating their room – it will only break your heart when the new, expensive wallpaper you painstakingly put up is covered in posters and ripped by sellotape. And even if you both decide on a scheme, chances are they will want to change it in a year or two! Bearing all this in mind, the room we eventually created is deliberately not finished. Instead, we have given Rachel a framework for her future style and ideas. At present she is all 'girl power', but this phase will blend into the next and the room needs to be able to make that transition without needing another overhaul.

To Rachel, like most people her age, her bedroom isn't just a place to sleep. It's a den. She keeps all her things in it; it's a place where she can get away from the rest of the family, and where she can entertain her friends. Her friends often come round to visit and they like to listen, and dance, to music. It was important to Rachel that there would be room to dance in the new bedroom, and space

Posters had been used to cover up the decor rather than contribute to it (*left*).

There was nothing to be done except strip the room bare (*right*).

Rachel wanted bare floorboards for dancing on, so we took up the old carpet and painted the boards black and green (*left*).

We added simple shelving, packed with jam jars, to house Rachel's large jewellery collection, and a full-length mirror as she was starting to get into clothes (*left*).

for her friends to sleep over. She also wanted a desk or table – somewhere she could do her homework.

### The bed and the door

Having the bed in the middle of the room takes up lots of space, and Rachel didn't like the wardrobes, so there was only one way to go – rip it all out and start again! I had heard of a firm who made scaffolding into bunk beds, so we called them in to make one to fit in the wall recess. Raising the bed gave us room to add a desk, which Rachel can use for her homework. It occurred to me that if we built the bed over the door we would maximise floor space, so I asked if I could cut the door in half, which we thought would be a cool thing to do. We bought a cheap door to replace the one already there, and cut the new one in half, just in case anybody changed their minds later! We eventually painted the door to match the walls, so the top half, which wouldn't be used, would blend into the background. The door is perfectly Rachel-sized, so any adults coming in will have to stoop to get in.

We attached a cork board, with a blue, wood border, all around the middle of the walls – a stylish place to put posters, pictures and cards (*left*).

The bed and ladder, specially created from scaffolding, were raised above the half-size door (*opposite*).

## Painting stripes on walls

• **craft knife** • **mini roller** • **roll of 1cm/½in low-tack masking tape** • **selection of vinyl matt emulsion paints**

**1** Wrap strips of masking tape around your roller, leaving 2.5cm/1in gaps between each strip. We used three strips of tape for our roller. Using a craft knife, cut either side of the strips down to the metal bar. Cut away the foam between the strips of tape and discard. It helps if you first rub the tape on your hand to remove some of the stickiness.

**2** Bind the sections between each section of foam with masking tape to keep the foam separate.

**3** Pour your paint into paint trays and roll the roller in the paint. Start by rollering on a piece of card. This will ensure the paint is evenly distributed. When you feel confident, roller your stripes onto the wall.

### The walls

We stripped off the wallpaper and painted the walls and ceiling pure white, to create a blank canvas. What it needed was a dash of colour. We bought small tins of blue, yellow, pink, red and lime green emulsion and painted fashionable 'go-faster' stripes all over using an adapted roller sponge (see box). I have no doubt that Rachel will want to change the look of the room in the future, so by adding areas of colour rather than painting a whole wall, she can easily paint over them and change the look in years to come.

I painted a large 'target' using string and a drawing pin as a compass. We also painted squares and crosses of colour,. The thing to do is let your imagination run riot, and be bold!

We added a cork board all the way round the middle of the walls.

You can't escape children and teenagers wanting to put up pictures, posters and postcards, but we thought this would be a neater, more stylish way of doing it. We glued the pieces of cork board directly onto the wall, so no screws were needed. We added a blue-painted, wood moulding onto the top and bottom of the board to give it a neat, finished effect. We left Rachel to arrange her posters.

## Customising picture frames

You could transform any old wooden frames you already have, or buy inexpensive new ones.

- wood picture frames • newspaper vinyl matt emulsion paint • glue gun and glue sticks • variety of decorations such as flowers, glitter, straws, buttons • drawing pins

**1** Remove the glass and backing from your frames to protect them while you work on the frame edge.

**2** Put down plenty of newspaper, and then paint the frames. We used the same paints we used for the wall patterns. Leave to dry.

**3** If you are using artificial flowers, start by cutting off the flower head close to the base of the flower head, so you have a fairly flat surface to attach to the frame. Use drawing pins to attach the flower heads to the frame. To make the glitter frames, apply the glue liberally, and scatter the glitter all over. Shake the frame to remove the excess glitter.

**4** Leave the frames to dry.

**5** Replace the glass, add your picture, and hang on the wall!

### The floor

The carpet didn't go with our new scheme, so we decided to take it up. Rachel also preferred the idea of floorboards for dancing – we'll have to see if people sitting below will feel the same! The floorboards underneath were in good condition, so were ideal for painting. After sanding them, we painted alternate floorboards green and black using water-based, wood floor dyes. These have revolutionised floor painting. They come in all colours and dry very quickly, which is ideal – no more waiting for hours watching paint dry. And there is no need to varnish them, unless you want a very shiny finish.

### The cushions

Piles of cushions were essential, so Rachel and her friends could lounge about when they were listening to music. We bought a few simple cushions and went mad adding tassels, stripes, and various shapes. Everything we made was done without sewing – much quicker and easier. We simply

Go-faster stripes and decorated picture frames cover the walls, both easy ways to achieve this "girl-power" look (*left and right*).

Piles of cushions, of various sizes, decorated with tassels and fringes, provide a comfy place for friends to lounge and sleep (*left*).

glued everything we wanted straight onto the cushions using a glue gun. These are great gadgets, but you do need to be very careful with them as the glue is extremely hot and can burn. The larger cushions are actually futon cushions which can be removed from their covers and used when Rachel's friends come to sleep over.

## The finishing touches

We added a full length mirror as Rachel has started to get into clothes. Rachel has lots of jewellery and she needed somewhere to put it all, so we put up some very simple shelves which we filled with decorated jam jars. We added a bit of interest to an inexpensive, simple lampshade by

carefully cutting out stars using a stanley knife. The final touch was to add a couple of bendy snake lights around the room. This enables Rachel to light areas of her room wherever she wants, which is especially useful above her desk, where the bed makes it a little dark. She can also use them as disco spot lights!

Rachel Pilkington
'It's fantastic!
Brilliant!'

# Children's

# OOM

**N**ot many of us have the luxury of being able to devote a whole room as a playroom, but many families see the benefit of having a safe place for their children to play and to keep toys. The Gowers are lucky because they have a large loft which is currently under-used.

Many of the ideas on the following pages would also work well for a young child's bedroom.

*Alison Gower*

'The room in the loft was always what attracted us to this house, yet since moving in, nothing has been done about it – it's just a toy and junk room. Steven and I never had a playroom when we were little and we would dearly love to convert the loft into one for our children.'

*Lesley Taylor*

'Loft space is often underused, which is a shame, as it can often be converted very easily, and used as an extra room. With a young family, the Gowers need all the space they can get!'

**A**lison and Steven Gower have three children; Matthew (4), Laura (2) and Timothy (5 months). They have a wonderful attic room, which they feel could be put to much better use. At the moment it is used to store toys and household junk, but Alison and Steven would like it to be used as a playroom for their three young children. When I first saw the room, it was quite dark and gloomy, but I felt that with the right choice of colours and by making the most of the light from the only window, it could become a pleasant room in which the children could play.

My first concern was of safety because the room was accessed by steep stairs, and there was only a little banister running along the side of the stairwell. We needed to add extra safeguards to ensure the children would not fall down the stairs. I decided to add a clear perspex panel above the banister, which would act as a safety barrier, and would also allow the daylight through. We also added a small gate at the top of the stairs.

Once the question of safety was addressed, we had to decide on a theme for the room. Playrooms, and children's rooms in general, are ideal places in which to let imaginative designing run wild. The occupants of such a room are normally the key to the best theme, and in this case, Matthew (the eldest) loves trains, so this gave me the starting point for my design.

### The station
The room was long and narrow so I decided to add some form of partition or divider to break up the room and

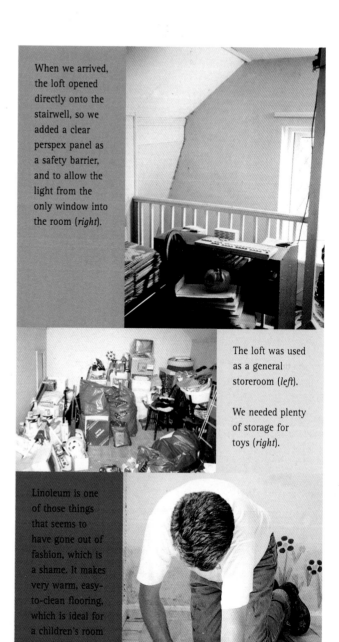

When we arrived, the loft opened directly onto the stairwell, so we added a clear perspex panel as a safety barrier, and to allow the light from the only window into the room (*right*).

The loft was used as a general storeroom (*left*).

We needed plenty of storage for toys (*right*).

Linoleum is one of those things that seems to have gone out of fashion, which is a shame. It makes very warm, easy-to-clean flooring, which is ideal for a children's room (*right*).

## Painting 'cartoon' flowers

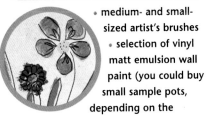

- medium- and small-sized artist's brushes
- selection of vinyl matt emulsion wall paint (you could buy small sample pots, depending on the number of flowers you wish to paint)
- black marker pen

**1** Start by painting green stems and leaves on the wall using a small artist's paint brush.

**2** To add the flower heads, dip the tip of a medium-sized artist's brush into your flower colour paint. Press the end of the brush flat against the wall to create a petal shape.

Repeat three times to get a tulip effect. Alternatively, start with a flower centre, and then when dry, add petals around.

**3** When the paint is dry, draw an outline around each petal using a marker pen. Also outline the stem and any flower centres. This creates the 'cartoon' effect.

give it extra width. This would create a room within a room, which would add interest for the children. As the theme was trains, I thought a station or ticket office was ideal. And as the room was quite dark, I thought that the remainder of the room could have an outdoor theme, giving it a spacious and airy appearance.

The first job was to build the partition. This was constructed from planed timber uprights and a frame, which ran along the ceiling and walls. We located the timber joists and nailed our timber uprights into these for strength. Once constructed, the partition was clad with pine tongue and groove, out of which the doorway

and two windows were cut. To add an authentic feel to the station, we added a pre-cut MDF pelmet along the roof area. The station was then ready to be painted. We used a vinyl soft sheen emulsion in dark cream.

We added two seating areas inside the station to emulate the layout of a traditional train. This meant that the children could pretend the building was both a train and a train station, and could put their toys into the storage room under the seated areas.

### The floor
The flooring needed to be practical, warm and in keeping with the theme of the room, so I chose sheet linoleum

in a grass green colour. Linoleum makes very warm, easy-to-clean flooring, which is ideal for a children's room. To make it a bit more interesting, we cut out stepping stone shapes. We used these as templates to cut pieces of charcoal-coloured linoleum, which we then fitted back into the green linoleum to create a stepping stone design up to the door of the station.

### The café
We added a small 'café' area outside the station. We thought that when the 'passengers' weren't waiting for the train, they could use the small garden tables and chairs for reading, drawing and playing.

## Dragging

We used a paint effect called 'dragging' to create the clouds on the ceiling and walls. Apply when your base coat is dry.

- selection of blue vinyl matt emulsion wall paints • acrylic scumble glaze
- large paint brush • large natural sponge
- dragging brush

1 In separate containers, mix your blue paints with acrylic scumble glaze.

2 Paint one coat of clear acrylic scumble glaze onto the surface you wish to paint. (The glaze has to be wet for the dragging effect to work, so do not delay doing the next stage.)

3 Using the various blue paint/acrylic scrumble glaze mixes and a

large paint brush, paint diagonal, jagged lines over the glazed surfaces.

4 Soften the edges of the lines by gently dragging them with a natural sponge.

5 Using a dragging brush, lightly blend the colours by moving the brush in a criss-cross motion. This creates the soft, cloudy effect.

### The walls and ceiling

The main room was given a coat of plain white, matt emulsion, over the walls and ceiling. This was to be the base for our main decoration scheme. We started by adding clouds to the ceiling and to the top half of the walls. This is quite simple. As long as you use the right type of paints, the effect will be light and airy. Below this, we sponged green paint onto the white walls to

emulate meadow land. When dry, we painted on leaves and flowers, aiming for a simple, crude look. We wanted to achieve a young, fun and almost 'cartoon' feel. On the opposite side of the room a small stone wall was created. This was made using small, domestic, cleaning sponges, rolled with brown paint and stamped on the wall. A tree was then hand-painted, made to look as though it were growing up behind the wall and up into the skyline. If you don't feel confident about painting freehand, do a light sketch in pencil first.

### The final touches

There was a small, ugly vent in the wall just behind the café area. The vent supplied air circulation to a chimney stack and could not be totally covered, so we attached a free-hanging sign to one of the branches on the painted tree. This meant that air could still circulate behind the sign, whilst the sign obscured the vent from view. We also added a couple of planters and window boxes, which we filled with artificial flowers.

Lighting was installed in the station with the use of battery powered small

This may look ambitious, but if you draw an outline in pencil first, it really isn't too difficult. Why not get the children to add their own flowers and leaves? (*left*)

We bought a real piece of fencing to make the safety gate at the top of the stairs (*right*). Ensure that it is well sanded before children touch it.

strip lights; these are ideal for the amateur 'DIYer'.

Storage for toys and games is important to keep the room as uncluttered as possible. We already had space under the station seats, but additional storage was created in the shape of wooden crates. We painted these and stamped them with the words 'This way up' and 'Fragile' to keep with the station theme. We also added some traditional 50s-style leather cases, found in a second hand store, and hung some hammocks – a fun way to store cuddly toys.

## Sponging

**We used this sponging technique to create the brick wall effect. Start by laying down plenty of newspaper – this can get very messy!**

● newspaper to lay on the floor ● 2 decorator's sponges ● small paint roller ● selection of vinyl matt emulsion wall paints (we used reds and browns to get our brick effect)

**1** Pour a little of your paints onto their tin lids. Using just one roller, roll the paints onto your sponge one by one, so you get a dappled, layered effect.

**2** Carefully place the sponge horizontally on the wall and press lightly. Remove the sponge to reveal the brick effect. Repeat this action over several rows to create the wall.

**3** To achieve the 'capping' effect on the top of the wall, cut your second decorator's sponge in half. Using one of these halves and your whole sponge (vertically this time), print alternately.

**The Gower family**

'We love it. It isn't at all how we imagined it to be, or how we would ever have done it ourselves. The children are very lucky; they'll be the envy of all their friends. The overall effect of clouds, railway station and café has given each of the children something to entertain them and a wonderful room to play in.'

# S T U D

# Y

**N**ot all homes have room for a study, but many of us need room to work – whether simply doing the household bills or actually working from home. The challenge for this room was to design and decorate a room that could be used primarily as a study, but could also be used as a spare bedroom.

Lucy, Andy and Patrick Thomas

'The room was a real mess, the dominant feature being those capacious yet dull, white bookcases. We wanted a functional study for when either of us needed to work from home, but with the flexibility to use it as a guest bedroom. I'd like bold colours, with none of the fussy swags I associate with interior decoration.'

Catherine Woram

'This room looked small and very, very cluttered, but it was the clutter – shelves stuffed with books, magazines, tapes and boxes – that made the room seem small.'

**L**ucy and Andy wanted the room to serve a dual purpose. They needed an office, as Lucy, who had just had a baby, works from home, yet they also needed it to act as a spare room if guests came to stay. Obviously they didn't want to have to spend hours tidying up and shuffling around furniture every time they were having visitors, so the room had to be quick and easy to convert from its office to bedroom function.

### The colour scheme

Because the room was small and had a fairly low ceiling, I felt using white for three walls and the ceiling would maximise the feeling of space. However, I decided to paint the window wall, which featured a french window, a cornflower blue to add an extra dimension while still retaining the feeling of space.

The overall look I was after was neat and streamlined, and by painting the three walls white, while using bold splashes of colour elsewhere, I could make it bright and cheerful without being at all distracting or overly busy.

### The floor

Lucy and Andy had wanted sisal flooring, and I found a soft option with a pure wool version. This was still practical yet was softer underfoot – important as the room was being used as an occasional bedroom, and also as baby Patrick was quite likely to crawl in when Lucy was working.

### The shelves

Working from home always tends to lead to a massive accumulation of files, reference material and numerous other

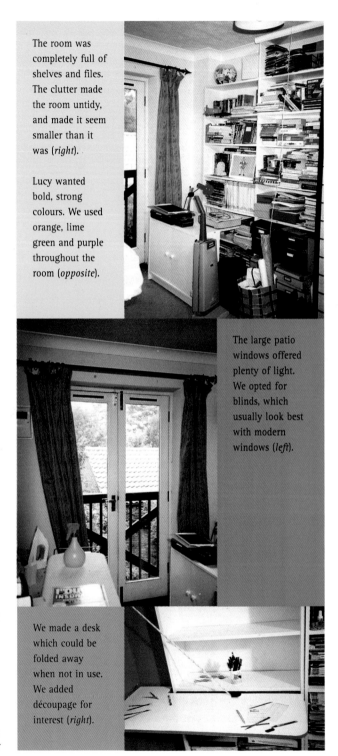

The room was completely full of shelves and files. The clutter made the room untidy, and made it seem smaller than it was (*right*).

Lucy wanted bold, strong colours. We used orange, lime green and purple throughout the room (*opposite*).

The large patio windows offered plenty of light. We opted for blinds, which usually look best with modern windows (*left*).

We made a desk which could be folded away when not in use. We added découpage for interest (*right*).

messy but vital pieces of paper, so a great deal of storage space was absolutely vital. However, the shelves totally dominated the room and took up far too much valuable floor space, so some of them had to go. Obviously I couldn't just dump the shelves and books, so our solution was to move them all to the spacious toilet room.

### The furniture

The lack of floor space was a major consideration in the design of the study. To save space the desk chair was provided with a handy hook to allow it to be hung up and I designed a desk which could be folded flat against the wall when not in use. To make the desk really different

and personal I decorated it using découpage techniques (see box) and a copy of the page from Lucy's diary dated the day the baby arrived.

Aside from the work aspect, the room was also going to be used as an occasional bedroom. A sofa bed was perfect for this dual purpose, as it would look smart, be useful as seating during the day, yet could be pulled out at night with ease.

I chose a neat and compact little sofa bed covered in navy blue cotton. Piled high with cushions decorated with the same simple motif of coloured squares (see box) used elsewhere in the room, the sofa looked inviting yet smart and totally in keeping with both the office and bedroom functions.

### Decorating the blinds

**This is a simple way to jazz up blinds.**

• bondaweb • material • iron and ironing board • scissors

**1** Place strips of bondaweb on the material, with the paper side out, and iron to fix the glue.

**2** Cut the material, with the bondaweb attached, into the shape you require. We used 10cm (4in) squares.

**3** Peel off the backing paper from the bondaweb and place the cut out piece of material bondaweb-side down, carefully onto the blinds.

**4** Again, iron the squares to fix the glue.

## Painting the squares

This is a very easy and inexpensive way to add interest to painted walls. As you don't need much paint for the squares, you could use a small sample pot.

• masking tape • tape measure • vinyl matt emulsion paint in two colours of your choice • medium paintbrush • cardboard • pencil • fine paintbrush

**1** Mask off a square on the wall measuring 80cm (3ft), though this can be smaller or larger depending on the size of the wall.

**2** Fill in the square with your choice of background paint. It is a good idea to use a fine paint brush to outline the squares, and then fill using a medium paintbrush. This gives you more control of your painting. Leave to dry.

**3** Cut a piece of cardboard to 10 x 10cm (4 x 4in) to act as a template for the smaller squares.

**4** On one side of your painted square, mark out two smaller squares by drawing around the cardboard cut-out with a pencil.

**5** Carefully mask off around the two smaller squares using masking tape.

**6** Fill in the masked-off squares with your second paint colour using a fine paintbrush.

**7** Leave the painted squares to dry thoroughly before removing the masking tape, to avoid chipping.

### The blinds

As the general clutter of work is hardly conducive to a peaceful night's sleep, a way had to be devised to disguise the books and files, bursting out of the shelves, when the room was being used a bedroom. I found some lovely lime green cotton roller blinds which could be pulled down to hide them. We decorated them with simple orange cotton squares that were applied with bondaweb – an easy, quick alternative to the drudgery of a needle and thread (see box).

Looking at the window, it struck me that I could also use roller blinds there instead of the curtains. They would match the ones covering the bookshelves, providing a unifying element, and wouldn't take up any floor or wall space – unlike the curtains which had filled that wall previously.

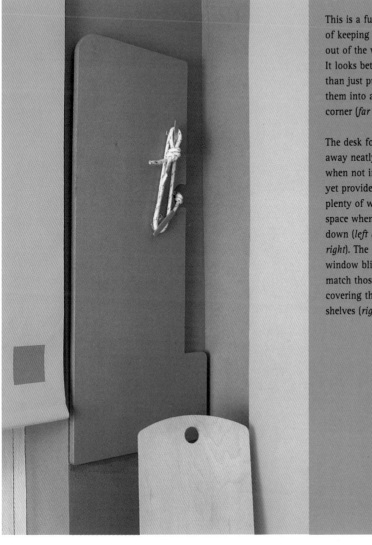

This is a fun way of keeping chairs out of the way. It looks better than just pushing them into a corner (*far left*).

The desk folds away neatly when not in use, yet provides plenty of work space when down (*left and right*). The window blinds match those covering the shelves (*right*).

## Découpage

Look through magazines, wallpaper samples, wrapping paper and books for pictures to use for découpage. We used pictures of pens and pencils, and a copy of the page from Lucy's diary on the day Patrick was born.

- selection of images • scissors or scalpel
PVA glue • acrylic clear varnish
- varnishing brush

**1** Cut out your images carefully using scissors or a scalpel.

**2** Start by arranging the images over the surface you want to decorate.

**3** Taking each image in turn, coat the back of each with glue then carefully, but firmly, smooth down. Wipe away any excess glue.

**4** When all your images are completely dry, varnish over the entire surface to protect your découpage design.

### The decoration

While keeping the design simple I felt that some decoration was needed. One cheap and very striking alternative to a framed poster or print was to create a simple, painted design, co-ordinated to match the design and colours used elsewhere, most notably on the blinds.

I masked off a large square on the wall and filled it in with the same cornflower blue paint as the window wall. When this was dry I painted two smaller squares in bright orange paint.

All of these ideas and techniques couldn't be easier to follow and could be adapted to many other rooms, such as a playroom which doubles as an occasional bedroom, or even a kitchen which also acts as a dining room. The aim is to keep things as simple and uncluttered as possible.

*Lucy Thomas*
'I feel that we've gained a room, which I thought of as little more than a cupboard before. Now that it's been fixed up, we really use it, both for working from home and for the ironing! The shelves are still choc full of books, but the beauty is that we can hide it all away when anyone comes round and the room quickly looks very minimal.'

# BATHR

# O O M

**B**athrooms need to be practical places, but they can also be very relaxing. Zoe and James hadn't had time to decorate their bathroom, so when we arrived it was anything but welcoming! Jocasta opted for a warm, rosy red colour scheme which completely transformed the room. Complete with books and a comfy chair, this bathroom is now a retreat!

**Zoe Hines**

'James works all week and I work all weekend, so we just haven't had time to do our bathroom yet. The rest of the house is fine – but we'd really appreciate some help with the bathroom.'

**Jocasta Innes**

'As bathrooms go, this was a good size, so we had plenty of room to work with. Zoe and James said they were happy for us to do absolutely anything we wanted.'

Decoratively speaking, this room was a mess. The wallpaper was peeling away, there was a mish-mash of carpeting and a rather nasty melamine-finished bath surround and vanity unit. The team moved in and stripped everything bare, removing all the wallpaper and carpets.

The bathroom is *en suite* with the master bedroom, but Zoe and James were happy for it to be different to their bedroom. The room was overwhelmed by a towering shelf, which ran alongside the bath, and acted as a room divider. It looked rickety and untidy, and made the bathroom look smaller than it actually was, so we decided to knock it down. It wasn't part of the structure, so we simply used large hammers, and bashed it down. When this was removed, we were left with a large, light space to work with.

## The walls

The units were basically sound, so I thought we would give them a new lease of life using paint. Zoe said she fancied a crimson room. I thought this might look a bit heavy, especially if in an emulsion, but I thought we could work with the idea. I decided a rosy red colourwash would work well, because it looks warm and pretty, without being heavy like a solid emulsion colour. Bathrooms usually only have one window, if they have a window at all, and it is important not to chose a dark colour which may make the room look small and dark. The rosy colour I had in mind did not absorb too much natural light, so would be ideal. I couldn't find the exact colour, so I mixed my own using a deep red/brown with a bit of purple.

Zoe and James hadn't had time to decorate their bathroom, and it felt cold and unwelcoming (*right*).

They had started to strip off the wallpaper, but had run out of enthusiasm (*left*). We finished the job, then lined the walls.

We wanted to make more of this large window (*right*).

We filled the glass shelves with perfume bottles and candles to add a touch of luxury. Just imagine how relaxing it would be to have a candlelit bath... (*right*).

We didn't have time to strip the walls, but if you have time, it is a good idea. We lined the walls with a heavy-duty lining paper which covers a multitude of sins, including odds and ends of old wallpaper and any small cracks and irregularities. We gave the paper a quick coat of wallpaper paste (size), followed by a non-absorbent base coat. We then applied the red colourwash. You need to apply the colourwash in uneven, random strokes to get a nice, soft effect. Keep the brush moving so you don't get any splodges of paint. I suggest you rope in a friend to help you!

We stencilled a feather design in off-white to give a delicate pattern to the walls and tiling (see box overleaf). The bathroom contained a cupboard, which housed the hot water tank for the house, and doubled as an airing cupboard. We painted it in the same way as the walls to disguise it.

The transformed bathroom (*left*).

We added framed prints to the walls, which added interest (*right*).

## Stencilling

There are hundreds of stencil designs available in the shops, or you could try making your own. This one is available from Jocasta's own stencil collection.

- 1m/3ft cardboard square • stencil
- masking tape • emulsion paint • saucer
- stencilling brush • newspaper

### The vanity unit

I chose a dark grey, pewter finish paint for the melamine vanity unit. We first prepared the melamine surface with a binding agent which allows water based paint to adhere to plastic surfaces. You leave this to dry, and then apply your choice of paint. A dark colour seemed the right choice here, to offset the prettiness of the rest of the room, as Zoe's husband will be using this bathroom too! We added one coat of polyurethane varnish which had a graphite powder in it, and this gave the unit an attractive, metallic sheen.

### The tiles

Tiles are expensive and tricky to replace, so we decided to paint them instead, and this is a very easy way of transforming them. Even textured or patterned tiles can be painted without too much difficulty. We painted ours to match the walls. We used the same binding agent we had used on the units to cover the black tiles which lined the recess above the basin. Then we used our rosy-coloured paint to paint all of the tiles. We used the same technique again when we added a few tiles around the top of the bath where we'd removed the partition shelving.

1 Decide where you are going to paint your stencil design. We used a large square of cardboard, to mark out square areas on the wall, in which to place the stencils. Work from one corner of the room, and mark the tip of each corner. This would be the point where the top of each stencil area would be. Using a square ensures the designs will be evenly spaced apart.

2 Attach the stencil to the wall, within one of your squares, using masking tape, or, if there are two of you, one of you can hold it in position against the wall, while the other applies the paint.

3 Tip a little paint onto a saucer. Dip the stencilling brush into the saucer and blot onto newspaper. Your brush should be almost dry before stencilling. Apply the paint within the stencil lightly to ensure that the paint does not bleed beyond the confines of the stencil and to create a soft finish. Try not to get too much paint on the stencil itself; if you do, carefully wipe the stencil.

4 Lift the stencil, and repeat the process in all the other marked positions. Be careful not to brush against the ones you have already done!

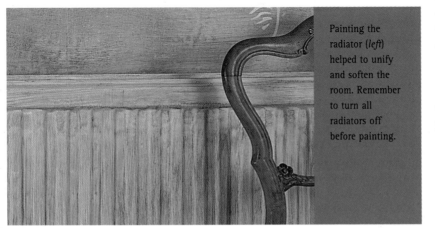

Painting the radiator (*left*) helped to unify and soften the room. Remember to turn all radiators off before painting.

We continued the stencil design over the airing cupboard, which helped to disguise it (*left*).

The finished bathroom looks warmer and more welcoming. The mirrors help to make the room look larger (*right*).

## The floor

The floorboards were in good condition, so we sanded these down to show off the grain. It's vital that you remove any splinters and bumps, especially as people will be walking around with bare feet. We then applied a diluted, subtle grey colourwash to create a bleached, driftwood finish. Simply apply this along each plank, going with the grain, using a large sponge. When dry, we varnished the floor to seal and protect it, and the room instantly looked more 'together'.

Wooden floors can actually be very warm, but if you can't bear the thought of stepping out of the bath or shower onto a wooden floor, there are plenty of warm, soft rugs available. Try to find one which has a non-slip underlay. If you have a small bathroom, you might be lucky and find an off-cut piece of carpet that fits.

## The mirrors

There was already a mirrored cabinet above the basin, which we thought would be useful to keep. I added a sheet of mirror glass above the basin, to create a mirror that went right up to the ceiling. This made a big difference to the room, adding sparkle and reflection everywhere. We added a 12cm/5in strip of mirror all round the top of the walls, 5cm/2in below the ceiling, which looked very pretty and intensified the sparkle effect. We had the glass cut for us, and we glued it straight onto the wall. You have to ensure that the wall is absolutely flat so the glue will adhere.

We made the existing mirrored recess at the wall end of the bath more of a feature (and more useful) by putting glass shelves across to hold talc, bath salts, perfume bottles etc. The existing tiles around the mirror alcove were painted in the same way as those around the cubby-hole above the basin.

## The finishing touches

The pipes behind the toilet were hidden by installing a simple box made out of MDF, which we painted to match the walls. We also added a small shelf above the toilet.

We moved the existing full length cream curtains to the side of the window to soften a boring corner, and replaced them with a very simple cream blind which was more practical, took up less room, and gave privacy to the room.

We fitted a simple light above the basin, and finally, we added a new light switch tassel, a bath mat, some beautiful prints, a few books for reading in the bath and some new, fluffy towels.

*Zoe Hines*
'We are both delighted
with our bathroom.
Our 4-year-old
William protested,
but that's because
he's a typical boy,
and just hates pink!'

## STOCKISTS AND SUPPLIERS

All prices and details were correct
at the time of publication.

### Special thanks to:

• **Do It All Ltd** For professional advice on any
decorating project, and details of nearest stores,
call the Do It All freephone Helpline (Mon to Sat
9am to 8pm; Sun 10am to 4pm) on 0800 436 436.
• **Black & Decker** Leading manufacturers of
power tools. For details of stockists and general
enquiries Tel: 0345 230 230
• **Stanley Tools** Manufacturers of quality hand
tools and decorating products. General
Enquiries Tel: 0114 276 8888
• **Dulux Paints** Dulux Advice Centre for all
enquiries Tel: 01753 550 555
• **Cotswold Outdoor Adventure Equipment**
Customer Services Tel: 01285 643 434
• **H.S.S Hire Service Group PLC** Group Office,
25, Willow Lane, Mitcham, Surrey CR4 4TS.
Tel: 0181 260 3100, Fax: 0181 687 5005
• **Singer UK Ltd** Customer Services
Tel: 0181 261 3230
• **Dickies UK Ltd** Protective clothing.
Tel: 01761 410041, Fax: 01761 414825
• **Ford Motor Co. Ltd** 2.3 litre 16 valve Galaxy.
For your nearest dealer call 0345 231231
• **Vauxhall** Omega Tourer and Highroof 2.5D.
For your nearest dealer call 0800455466
• **LDV** Hi Loader. For your nearest dealer call
0800 400407.
• **Plascon International Ltd** DIY retail specialist
paint. Tel: 01703 226 722, Fax: 01703 231 766
• **London Graphics Centre** Fine art and
graphics materials. Tel: 0171 240 0095,
Fax: 0171 831 1544
• **Pentonville Rubbers** Converters of foam and
rubber to any size or shape. Tel: 0171 837 4582

### Hallway

• **Paint Magic Ltd** 79 Shepperton Road,
Islington, London, N1 3DF. Tel: 0171 354 9696,
Fax: 0171 226 7760

• **Trowbridge Gallery** 555 Kings Road, London,
SW6 2EB. Tel: 0171 371 8733, Fax: 0171 371 8138
*prints (£180 large, £160 small)*
• **Mark Griffiths Woodwork** Unit 4, Sewells
Farm, Barcombe, East Sussex, BN41 1XF.
Tel: 01273 401 611
*finial (£50)*
• **Natural Flooring Direct** Natural Flooring
Direct, Freepost Lon 1229, London, SE16 4BR.
For information telephone: 0800 454 721
*Sisal mini boucle maize carpet (£40 per sqm)*
• **Culm Valley Weavers** Specialist Commission
Weavers. Units C1/C2 Dunkeswell Business
Park. Dunkeswell, Honiton, Devon, EX14 ORA.
Tel/Fax: 01404 891898
*stair carpet (under £40 per metre)*
• **Carpet Accessory Trims Ltd** Unit 24C, Park
Avenue Estate, Sundon Park, Luton, LU3 3BP.
Tel: 01582 561 500, Fax: 01582 561 900
*stair rods including all fittings (around £200)*
• **Floor Coverings International Carpet Fitters**
Tel: 0800 22 99 33
• **First Action Plumber** Tel: 0181 679 0666
(price on application)
• **Glass Express** 56-58 Lupus Street, London,
SW1 3EN. Tel: 0171 828 6046,
Fax: 0171 834 0017
*mirrors and glass (prices on application)*

### Lounge

• **Wm. O'Hanlon and Co.** Tel: 01686 624444
*velvet for curtains (around £15 per metre)*
• **Chapham Glynn Fabrics** Unit 1,
73 Norlington Road, Leyton, E10 6LA.
Contact John Watkins Tel: 0181 558 7705
*sofa throws (under £15 per metre)*

• **GP and J Baker** Tel: 01494 467467
*cushion materials (prices £30-80 per metre)*
• **Pentonville Rubbers**
*cushion pads (prices on request)*
• **Stampability** Tel: 0116 254 7671
*heraldic stamp kit used on cushions (under £10)*
• **New Century Cleaning Company**
Tel: 0171 735 7151, Fax: 0171 820 1030
(Minimum charge is £40 to clean a room)
• **The Pier** Specialists in unusual dressing for
around the home. Tel: 0171 814 50041
*frames (£5-25), church candles (£2-13),
candle sticks (£3.50 - £15)*
• **The Futon Company Ltd** Tariff Road, London,
N17 OEB. Tel: 0181 365 0771, Fax: 0181 365 0881
*futon cushions (plain £50, leopard print £70).*
• **Decorative Fabrics Gallery Ltd**
278 Brompton Road, London, SW3 2AS.
Tel: 0171 589 4778, Fax: 0171 589 4781
*cow print velvet cushion (under £70 per cushion)*
• **William Gee Ltd** Wholesalers and retailers of
textiles, haberdashery and trimmings.
520-522 Kingsland Road, London E8 4AH.
Tel: 0171 254 2451, Fax: 0171 249 8116
*trimming (prices on request)*
• **Karadia Trims** Wholesalers and retailers of
garment trimmings. Eastern Boulevard, (Corner
of Rydal Street), Leicester, LE2 7BF.
Tel: 0116 233 3434, Fax: 0116 233 3608
*sewing cottons (under £2 a cone for a minimum
order of 8 cones)*
• **Fantasy Fayre** General enquiries: 0171 916 2100
*fun fur (under £10 per metre)*
• **Halfords** Tel: 0345 626625.
*silver paint spray for shelf brackets (Ford Stratos
silver), white primer spray for shields (under £5)*

• **Polyvine** Range of paints for decorative effects contact customer services on 01454 261 276.
*gold paint for cornicing (£5 for small, £15 for large)*
• **Hammerite Products Ltd** Tel: 01661 830 000 Fax: 01661 835 760
*gold metallic paint for picture frame (under £10)*
• **Bar** Thanks to: Smirnoff, Drambuie, Archers, Disarrono Ammareto, Pommery champagne, Veuve Clicquot champagne, Laurent Perrier champagne, Courvoisier, Britvic, Johnny Walker, Heineken, Rolling Rock, Murphys Irish Stout, Boddingtons Bitter, Stella Artois, Southern Comfort, Gordons Gin, Gloag's Gin, Pernod, Highland Park 12 year Old Single Malt Scotch Whisky, Bunnahabhain Single Islay Scotch Malt Whisky,  Black Bottle Malt Whisky.
• **Comet** Call 0500 425 425 for nearest store details.
*Daewoo mini fridge (under £150)*
• **Swish Ltd** Manufacturer of curtain poles, tracks and window accessories. Lichfield Road Industrial Estate, Tamworth, Staffordshire, B79 7TW. Tel: 01827 64222 242
*System 1 curtain pole (under £20)*
• **Dylon** Consumer advice line (advice on dying techniques and stockists) Tel: 0181 663 4296.
*olive green fabric dye (under £5)*
• **British Trimmings** Retailers and wholesalers of decorative trimmings. Tel: 0161 480 6122
*tie backs (prices range from £10-50)*

## Kitchen
• **Harcros Timber & Building Supplies Ltd** Harcros House, 1, Central Road, Worcester Park, Surrey KT4 8DN. Tel: 0181 255 2289 Fax: 0181 255 2280
*timber for corner cupboard (prices on request)*
• **Crosts & Assinder Ltd** General Enquiries Tel: 0121 622 1074
*cabinet door knobs (under £3), door handles (under £7)*
• **Plascon International Ltd** *tile primer (under £9 for 750ml)*
• **Pebeo** Decorative Paint Specialists General Enquiries Tel: 01703 901 914
*liquid crystal glass paint (under £3 per 45ml)*

• **Junckers Ltd** Specialists in hardwood floors and worktops. Tel: 01376 534 710
*worktop available in steamed and unsteamed beech (from £450-700)*
• **Rustins Ltd** Manufacturers of wood finishes, speciality paints and DIY sundries. Tel: 0181 450 4666, Fax: 0181 452 2008
*wood bleach (under £9 per wood bleaching kit)*
• **A.E.G.** *Oven "Competence 5231B" (under £600), hob "934 1OG" (under £300), cooker hood "115D" (under £150)*
For a brochure: Tel: 01635 572 720
• **Carron Phoenix** Manufacturers of stainless steel and composite sinks. Stenhouse Road, Carron, Falkirk, FK2 8DW. Tel: 01324 638321
*sink (prices range from £75-300)*
• **Lakeland Ltd** Retailers of Creative Kitchenware Alexandra Buildings, Windermere, Cumbria, LA23 IBQ. Tel: 01539 488 100
*creative kitchenware (prices on request)*
• **Freeman's** (For a mail order catalogue call freephone number 0800 900 200)
• **Dulux paints accessories**
Matt Emulsion for stencilling and Satinwood for woodwork (Cream 45 YY 75/110)
Matt Emulsion (Blue 31 BB 23/340)
Matt Emulsion (Orange 83 YR 44/540)

## Dining room
• **Natural Fabric Company** Specialists in natural utility fabrics. Tel: 01488 684 002, Fax: 01488 686 455
*material on walls (under £2 per metre, width 127cm)*
• **Dulux paints**
Matt emulsion (Blue 91 BB 14/430)
Matt emulsion (Pure brilliant white)

• **YKK (U.K.) Ltd** Customer Service, (Northern) Tel: 01928 593 800, Fax: 01928 593 819, (Southern) Tel: 0171 253 2077, Fax: 0171 250 0048
*hook and loop (under £30 per 25m reel)*
• **Freudenberg Nonwovens LP** PO Box 3, Greetland, Halifax, West Yorkshire, HX4 8JN Tel: 01422 313131 Fax: 01422 313142
*wunda web bumper pack (under £15)*
• **Valiant Lamps Ltd** 20 Lettice Street, Fulham, London, SW6 4EH. Contact: 0171 736 8115
*Gerard Sudron candle lights (under £5 per bulb)*
• **Torbay Electrical Installations** 20 Brunswick Terrace, Torre, Torquay, Devon, TQ1 4AE. Tel: 01803 312 645 Fax: 01803 312 645
*(price on application)*
• **Inn on the Green** Crooklets Beach, Bude, Cornwall, EX23 8NF. Tel: 01288 356 013 Fax: 01288 356 244
• **House of Fraser** Tel: 0171 963 2236.
*accessories*
• **Huck Pelacon UK Ltd** 1 Foundry Lane, Bridport, Dorset, DT6 3RP. Tel: 01308 425 100 Fax: 01308 458 109.
*netting (under £1 per square metre)*
• **The Discount Fabric Warehouse** 17-19 Wharf Street South, Leicester, LE1 2AA. Tel: 0116 251 2423 Fax: 0116 253 3080
*hessian (under £5 per metre)*
• **Freeman's** Tel: 0800 900 200.
*pillows (£20 per pair)*
• **Mark Griffiths Woodwork** Unit 4, Sewells Farm, Barcombe, East Sussex, BN41 1XF. Tel: 01273 401 611
*table legs (price on request)*
• **Jewson Ltd** Tel: 0800 539 766
*formica (under £70)*

## Music room

• **Daler Rowney Ltd** Fine art and graphics materials P.O.Box 10 Bracknell, Berkshire RG12 8ST. Tel: 01344 424 621, Fax: 01344 486 511
*acrylic paints* (burnt umber, raw umber and burnt sienna) (under £3 per 38ml)

• **Craig & Rose** Manufacturers of paints, varnishes and glazes. 172, Leith Walk, Edinburgh, EH6 5EB. Tel: 0131 554 1131
*glaze* (under £30 per 5 litres)

• **Dulux paints**
Vinyl silk emulsion (Pink 44YR 69/180)
Vinyl matt emulsion (Red 04YR 11/538)

• **Plascon International Ltd**
*matt black paint* (under £6 per 250ml), *red oxide primer* (£3.50 per 250ml)

• **Allied Carpets Ltd** Allied House, 76, High Street, Orpington, Kent, BR6 OJQ. For details of stockists Tel: 0800 192 192
*carpet* (prices on request)

• **Duralay** Tel: 01706 213 131
*underlay* (prices on request)

• **Jali Ltd** Decorative woodwork for the home Apsley House, Chartham, Canterbury, Kent CT4 7HT. Tel: 01227 831 710 Fax: 01227 831 950
*pelmet* (start at under £15 per 6 ft)

• **Pentonville Rubbers**
*cushion pads* (prices on request)

• **William Gee Ltd** Wholesalers and retailers of textiles, haberdashery and trimmings 520-522 Kingsland Road, London E8 4AH. Tel: 0171 254 2451, Fax: 0171 249 8116
*threads* (prices on request, brochure available)

• **Moss Bros.**
General enquiries Tel: 0171 447 7200
*evening suit* (prices on request)

• **Muir Hewitt** Art Deco Originals. Halifax Antiques Centre, Queens Road Mills, Queens Road/Gibbet Street, Halifax HX1 4LR. Tel/Fax: 01422 347 377
*accessories* (prices on request)

• **Do It All Ltd** circular wall lights and blinds

• **Rose Morris Music Store** 11 Denmark Street, London WC2H 8LS. Tel: 0171 836 0991 Fax: 0171 240 9874
*Bodhrans drums covering lights* (under £30)

• **W. Sitch & Co. Ltd** Art metal workers and manufacturers and dealers of electrical fittings 48, Berwick Street, Oxford Street, London W1V 4JD. Tel: 0171 437 3776 Fax: 0171 437 5706
*electrical gold silk flex* (under £4 per metre)

• **Rufflette Ltd** Leading manufacturers of curtain styling products. Sharston Road, Manchester M22 4TH. Tel: 0161 998 1811, Fax: 0161 945 9468
*curtain tape* (prices start at under £2 per metre)

• **Russell & Chapple Ltd** 23 Monmouth Street, Shaftesbury Avenue, London WC2H 9DE. Tel: 0171 836 7521
*fabric* (under £3 to under £6 per metre.)

• **Swish Ltd** Leading manufacturers of curtain poles, tracks and window accessories. Lichfield Road Industrial Estate, Tamworth, Staffordshire, B79 7TW. Enquiries Tel: 01827 642 242
*curtain track* (under £6)

• **Tracey Kendall** Silk screen printing on fabrics, wallpapers and flat surfaces of any size. Tel: 0181 769 0618
(prices on request)

• **Stuart Stevenson** 68, Clerkenwell Road, London EC1M 5QA. Tel: 0171 253 1693
*gold powders and bronzing medium* (prices start at under £3 per 25g)

• **London Graphics Centre**
*stencil card* (£3 per A1 sheet)

• **Scale Reprographics Ltd**
Contact: Mike Wright, Tel: 0171 407 3309
*enlargements* (prices on request)

• **South London Screens** Manufacturers and suppliers of silk screens and silk screen printing equipment. Contact: Keith Dent, Tel: 0181 694 8110
*silk screen* (prices on request)

## Master bedroom

• **Pebeo** Decorative paint specialists
General Enquiries Tel: 01703 901 914
*fabric paint for curtain stencils* (£3 per 45ml)

• **Carpet Services Ltd** 12, Cardiff Road, Taffs Well, Cardiff, CF4 7RA. Tel: 01222 810 351, Fax: 01222 813 026
*carpet fitting* (prices on request)

• **Cormar Carpets** Manufacturers of tufted carpets. General Enquiries Tel: 01204 882 241 (prices on request)

• **James Hare Silks** U.K's leading silk merchants General Enquiries 0113 243 1204
*curtain fabric* (Silk 31000 Colour 29) (under £6 per metre)

• **Edmund Bell & Co. Ltd** Converters of soft furnishing fabrics. Tel: 01274 680 000
*lining* (under £2 per metre)

• **Monkwell** Wholesalers of furnishing fabrics, trimmings and accessories. Tel: 01202 762 456
*muslin* (5194) *for sheer curtains.*

• **Rufflette Ltd** Manufacturers of curtain styling products. Sharston Road, Manchester M22 4TH. Tel: 0161 998 1811 Fax: 0161 945 9468
*curtain tape* (prices start at £2 per metre)

• **Harrison Drape** Window furnishing specialists Customer Services Tel: 0121 766 6111
*curtain poles and tracks* (prices on request)

• **Iron Art of Bath** Upper Lambridge Street, Larkhall, Bath, BA1 6RY. Tel: 01225 311 273 Fax: 01225 443 060
*wrought iron bedhead* cost £200 incl. VAT. (all handmade to order, prices on request)

• **Liberon Waxes Ltd**
General Enquiries Tel: 01797 367 555
*gilding cream* (£5 per 15ml pot)

• **London Graphics Centre**
*stencil card* (under £3 per A1 sheet)
• **Richard Burbidge Ltd** Manufacturers of timber-based home improvement products. Brochure Tel: 01691 678 214. Stockists Tel: 01691 678 201. Technical advice Tel: 01691 678 212
*wooden coving* (prices on request)
• **Attic Gallery** Specialists in Contemporary Welsh Art. 61, Wind Street, Swansea SA1 1EG. Tel: 01792 653 387
*paintings* (prices on request)
• **Solaglas Ltd** Glass, glazing and frame manufacturers and fitters. Tel: 01222 481 811
*wardrobe and dressing table mirrors* (prices on request)
• **Debenhams**
Customer Services Tel: 0171 408 4444
*Damask bedlinen* (from under £45), *100% cotton duvet covers* (from £30-60).
• **Dulux paints**
Once emulsion (Ivory Lace)
Satin wood (Carrara )
Special effects (Raw silk)
Vinyl matt emulsion (Amaretto)
Vinyl matt emulsion (Harvest beige)
Vinyl matt emulsion (Carrara)

## Child's bedroom
• **C.C. Galleries** Bespoke picture framers and ornate mirrors. Tel: 0181 980 2888
*picture frames* (from £20-30)
• **Futon Company** Tariff Road, London, N17 OEB. Tel: 0171 221 2032, Fax: 0181 365 0881
*futon cushions* (plain colours under £50, leopard print from under £70)
• **Santoro** Tel: 0181 241 2448
*ready-made cushions from the Passionart Collection* (prices range from £30-135)
• **Scaffold Services Ltd** Bedroom Furniture Hawarden Avenue, Leicester, LE5 4NN. Tel: 0116 276 8125
*scaffolding bed* (from around £225, made to order)
• **Kudhail Quilting Co.** Wholesale Textile Merchants. Tel: 0181 514 0605 for samples
*cushion fabrics* (prices start at £2 per metre)

• **Kurtex Textiles** Suppliers of Nylon & Cotton Lycra Fabrics. Tel: 0115 967 0770 for samples. (prices start at under £5 per metre)
• **Malabar** Suppliers of fine cotton and silk fabrics. Tel: 0171 501 4200 for samples. (prices start at under £35 per metre)
• **G.P. & J. Baker** For details of your nearest stockist contact: 01494 467 467 for samples.
*silks* (prices £30-80 per metre)
• **Monkwell** Wholesalers of furnishing fabrics, trimmings and accessories. General Enquiries Tel: 01202 762 456 for samples. (prices start at under £20 per metre)
• **Pentonville Rubbers**
*large floor cushion pads* (prices on request)
• **Morplan** Suppliers of fashion equipment and consumables. 56, Great Titchfield Street, London W1P 8DX. Mail Order Tel: 0800 435 333
*Rails* (from £20), *Hangers* (30p each)
• **Liberon Waxes Ltd**
General Enquiries Tel: 01797 367 555
*floorboard wood dyes* (prices from £5 for 250ml to £35 for 5 litres)
• **Debenhams**
Customer Services Tel: 0171 408 4444
*Duvet cover* (£25), *pillow cases* (£10)
• **Habitat** General Enquiries Tel: 0645 334 433 Contact sales department Tel: 0161 480 6122
*lime green paper lampshade* (from £10-20)
• **British Trimmings** Contact Sales Department Tel: 0161 480 6122
*accessories* (from £10-50)
• **Montgomery Interior Fabrics** Broughton Mill Road, Bretton, Chester CH4 OBY. Customer enquiry line Tel: 01244 661 432
*blinds* (from £50 upwards)

• **Bead Exclusive** Suppliers of 100s of beads from worldwide sources to wholesale and retail. 30, Seymour Road, Newton Abbot, Devon, TQ12 2PU. Tel: 01626 65481
*beads* (start at 2p each)
• **Sia U.K. Ltd** Pagoda Park, West Mead, Swindon, Wiltshire, SN5 7TT. Tel: 01793 488 558
*artificial flowers* (prices on request)
• **D.R. Jackson** Suppliers and fitters of all makes of carpet. Tel: 0161 941 4128
*carpet fitters* (prices on request)
• **C.E.A.** Domestic, Industrial & Commercial Electrical Contractors. Tel: 0161 654 7097
*electrician* (prices on request)
• **Do It All Ltd**
*pinboard, snake lights* and *t.v. wall bracket*
• **Dulux paints**
Vinyl matt emulsion:
(red 19YR 13/558)
(pink 51RR 62/190)
(green 90YY 48/650)
(blue 39BB 18/351)
(yellow 23YY 62/816)

## Playroom
• **Forbo-Nairn Ltd** Manufacturers of floor coverings: linoleum and cushioned vinyl Sales Desk Tel: 01592 643 777
*linoleum flooring* (for wholesale, under £12 per square metre)
• **Carpet Services Ltd** Suppliers, fitters and cleaners of all types of flooring. 12, Cardiff Road, Taffs Well, Cardiff, CF4 7RA. Tel: 01222 810 351, Fax: 01222 813 026
• **Pentonville Rubbers**
*foam for train seats* (prices on request)

• **William Gee Ltd** Wholesalers and retailers of textiles, haberdashery and trimmings. 520-522 Kingsland Road, London E8 4AH. Tel: 0171 254 2451 (prices on request, brochure available)

• **Plascon International Ltd** UK brand leader in DIY retail specialist paint. *blackboard paint* (under £6 per 250ml)

• **I.C.I. Acrylics** Manufacturers of perspex sheets, acrylic composites and lucite. General Enquiries Tel: 01254 874 444 *perspex* (prices on request)

• **Jali Ltd** Decorative Woodwork for the Home Apsley House, Chartham, Canterbury, Kent CT4 7HT. Tel: 01227 831 710, Fax: 01227 831 950 *decorative pelmet* (prices start at £15 per 6 ft.)

• **Dulux paints:**
Vinyl matt emulsion (Bright white)
Special effects (White veil)
Vinyl soft sheen (Clarence House)
Vinyl soft sheen (Hampton Court)

## Study

• **Natural Flooring Direct** Freepost Lon 1229, London, SE16 4BR. Tel: freephone 0800 454 721 *wool carpet* (Panama Spice) (under £40.00 per square metre (includes fitting)

• **The Holding Company Ltd** Suite 15, Imperial Studios, 3 -11 Imperial Road, London, SW6 2AG. Tel: 0171 610 9160, Fax: 0171 610 9166 *storage boxes* (all shown under £15)

• **Montgomery Interior Fabrics** Broughton Mill Road, Bretton, Chester CH4 OBY. Customer enquiry line: 01244 661 432 *Shaker plain blinds in lime green* (colourway 7). (Small blinds £70, large blind £300).

• **Freeman's** Tel: 0800 900 200. *sofa bed* (£200)

• **Lakeland Ltd** The creative kitchenware company. Alexandra Buildings, Windermere, Cumbria, LA23 1BQ. Customer Services: Tel: 015394 881 00, Fax: 015394 883 00 *wire storage rack* (£50)

## Bathroom

• **Paint Magic Ltd** 79 Shepperton Road, Islington, London, N1 3DF. Tel: 0171 354 9696, Fax: 0171 226 7760 *paint and paint brushes* (prices on request)

• **William Zinsser** 26 High Street, Pinner, Middlesex, HA5 5PW. Tel: 0181 866 9977. *primer* (under £10)

• **Marks and Spencers** Tel: 0171 935 4422 *towels* (from £5 to £25)

• **Caithness Glass** Inveralmond, Perth, Scotland, PH1 3TZ. Tel: 01738 637 373, Fax: 01738 622 494 *perfume bottles* (under £25, bowls from £30-50)

• **Montgomery Interior Fabrics**
*Roman blind in beige* (Norway, colourway 4) (£190)

• **Swish Ltd** Manufacturer of curtain poles, tracks and window accessories. Lichfield Road Industrial Estate, Tamworth, Staffordshire, B79 7TW. Tel: 01827 64222 242 *curtain poles* from Expressions range (£35)

• **Glass Express** 56-58 Lupus Street, London, SW1 3EN. Tel: 0171 828 6046, Fax: 0171 834 0017 *glazier* (prices on application)

• **Rapid Response** 15 Waldegrave Road, Anerley, London, SE19 2AR. Tel: 0181 406 5490 *electrician* (prices on application)

• **Skippy Nationwide** Tel: 0500 401 148 (prices available on request)

# ACKNOWLEDGEMENTS

Our team of workers couldn't have been more professional and great fun: the artistic and ever cheerful Claire and Prem, who missed out on many night's sleep to get an extra coat of paint on the walls; Nikki ('driller-killer'), the girl who, with a shrug of her shoulders, could be trusted with anything; Charlotte and Ashleigh, who with their sewing machines and tuneful voices would sing and sew cushions and curtains well into the early hours of the morning; Gary, with his winning smile, dangerous driving and desire to spend two months on a piece of furniture rather than the required two days; Annabell, our wonderful helper, who learnt more about sugar soap, brush strokes, baked potatoes and pasta in five weeks than anyone would want to know in a lifetime; and little Kristina, our work experience person and, yes, she did experience work. Last, but not least, the TV production team, Susan, Jo, Simone and Ann, who drove, cooked, baked, shopped, steamed, stripped, lent shoulders to cry on in the early hours, and always had a solution.